KILLING FOR PROFIT
The Social Organization
of Felony Homicide

MARY LORENZ DIETZ

Nelson-Hall nh Chicago

To Gram, Nikki, Leif and EvAnn, my family,
and in memory of Manfred Lorenz

LIBRARY OF CONGRESS CATALOGING IN PUBLICATION DATA

Dietz, Mary Lorenz.
  Killing for profit.

  Bibliography: p.
  Includes index.
  1. Murder—United States.   I. Title.
HV6529.D53   1983   364.1'523   82-24571
ISBN 0-8304-1008-2

Manufactured in the United States of America

10   9   8   7   6   5   4   3   2   1

The paper in this book is pH neutral (acid-free).

Contents

Preface

What's a nice lady like you . . . ? A personal note on the subject of violence and murder.

On learning that I teach and do research on violence and murder, people who know me as a college professor, a mother, or a baseball coach, usually express surprise and often horror that this should be my subject matter. Underlying this reaction I always sense the question, "What is a nice lady like you doing in an area like that and what could you possibly know about it?" I have not always been a college professor, mother, and baseball coach. I grew up hanging but on the streetcorners in Detroit and have lived most of my life here. My earlier research on violence was based on a participant observer knowledge of Detroit's violent subculture and many observations of street and domestic violence. For kids growing up in this city the gang fights and post dance and sports events altercations were a normal part of the scenario. I learned then how easy it is to fall into the kind of thinking that justifies violence and depersonalizes the victims. Since that time my observations of violence have extended to the parks and beaches, bars and restaurants, home and parking lots and have become a major part of my research interest.

My experience with murder has been in one way more removed. I have not witnessed murder although I have seen its immediate aftermath at crime scenes with the police and on the autopsy table at the morgue. In other ways, however, murders have affected me more than the other types of violence I have observed, as I have been close to both the killers and victims in a number of murder cases. The first case in which murder was no longer remote occurred when I was in high school and one of my friends was shot in a police chase. The three others who were in the car were charged with murder. Not many years after this another friend was charged with murder when she shot her husband after a beating. It was only two years later that my husband was shot by an armed robber he had tried to prevent from leaving the robbery scene. Each of these cases, especially the murder of my husband, affected me personally and profoundly. As I struggled to make sense of what seemed to be essentially senseless events, I began to wonder about the causes and meaning of violence in human life. When I returned to school to work on my Ph.D., my interest in crime and criminals focused more and more on the areas of violence and murder. The killings mentioned earlier happened many years ago, but even within the last few years four people I have known have been victims of felony homicides. In my own thinking I have moved from the belief that murder was beyond comprehension and beyond the control of the killers to an understanding of violence and murder within a framework of social interaction. I have moved from the idea that people who engage in violence are mentally ill and out of control to the belief that they are for the most part no different from everyone else, apart from their willingness to kill.

Mills has described for us how our public interests

develop from our private experiences and Weber has proposed that research is enriched by personal understanding. I believe that in my case both of these positions are valid. My personal experiences have provided the impetus for my research and have provided me with a deeper understanding of the significance of murder and the irreplaceability of human life. This is balanced by my knowledge of the people who engage in violence, which helps me to understand both the killers and victims as human beings and not merely cases in a study.

One of my colleagues on reading a draft of this study remarked to me that he found himself becoming blasé and taking even the most gruesome torture cases as "everyday" after a while. I noticed this response (or lack of response) among the police officers as well. Perhaps the response of people who are not involved gives us a clue to what happens to the killers in these cases as well as to others who are constantly exposed to news of killings. I hope that is not the experience of the readers of this study because I believe that the importance of murder must not be forgotten nor should the loss of both the victims and the killers to society be minimized. If the reader loses a sense of horror on reading these cases, this study will be worse than useless. On the other hand, the studies that deal with killers as less than human or as sets of figures allow the reader to depersonalize the reality just as the killer does. It is my hope that this study will raise questions and provoke thought and further research. For if we are ever to prevent violence and murder, we must first understand how they occur in human life. I will be satisfied if I have contributed in some small way to this understanding.

Acknowledgments

Without the cooperation and helpfulness of the Detroit Police Department, this study could not have taken place. In particular, the staff members of the Homicide Division, under the direction of Inspectors Robert Hislop and Gilbert Hill, were unfailingly supportive and willing to share their vast knowledge of homicide. My special thanks to Squad 7, the Felony Homicide Squad, and to Detectives Awe, Baginsky, Bulgin, Davies, Kimber, Knepp, McCarty, and Newcomb, from whom I learned so much. I also want to thank "David" and "Ricardo" and the other men who shared their experiences. I owe much to my friends and colleagues for their time and interest in this project, especially Bob Prus, Bob Whitehurst, Janice Drakich, and Jack Ferguson for their comments and advice and encouragement.

Thanks also to my typist, Kay Rice, for her gracious attitude and efficient work on many versions of this manuscript. I appreciate the Department of Sociology and Anthropology and the University of Windsor for encouraging and supporting this research and Aysan Tuzlak, Jill Marks, and David Hillock for their work on the data.

PART ONE

We drove around until morning. Looking for something. Looking for a way to make money. We came on this street and were looking at some houses and we stopped. We seen the side door open and we seen some garbage cans or something. We waited awhile, just stood there. An old guy 91 years old come out and best I can remember, we all rushed in. Me and two of the guys rushed downstairs and one other guy rushed upstairs. The old guy had fell down the stairs and Dwayne was down the basement askin' him where the money was. The old guy was just mumblin' and sayin' he didn't have no money so Dwayne started kickin' the guy and askin' for money. I said, "Hey, the guy is old. He can't take all that kickin'." But he kicked him a couple more times, askin' for money. . . .

("Was the old man alive when you left the house or did you ask later if he was dead?")

I didn't know. I never thought about it. It didn't matter.

(Interview with David)

1 Introduction to Felony Homicide

This book is about killing. It is about the kind of cold-blooded, impersonal, predatory murder that people fear most. We call this type of killing felony homicide.[1]

Felony homicide occurs during robberies and rapes. It includes contract killings arranged to get rid of business rivals or to collect insurance money. It also includes torture killing criminals inflict upon each other. We fear felony homicide most because it is an act over which we have no control and against which we have no defense. The victims are found in stores and houses, in streets and alleys, and in parking lots. The police usually have no leads such as quarrel or enmity, no relationships to investigate, no clues. The killers and victims are strangers or casual acquaintances.

The purpose of this book is to examine felony homicide, the particular type of murder that can be conceived as the ultimate form of violence. It may be distinguished

---

1. Felony murder in Uniform Crime Reporting is defined as those killings resulting from robbery, burglary, sex motive, gangland and institutional slaying, and all other felonious activities. Felony and suspected felony murders in 1976 constituted 28 per cent of all murders (Haskell and Yablonsky, 1976:96).

from other murders in a number of ways: (1) the killers in felony homicides are usually career criminals; (2) the context leading to the murder and often the murder itself involves planning and premeditation; (3) there tend to be more people involved, multiple victims and particularly multiple offenders; (4) the victims are often forcibly/physically restrained; (5) there is seldom a preceding argument.

THE INCREASE IN FELONY HOMICIDE

Crime has increased throughout the world in recent years (Radzinowicz and King, 1977). Violence has been particularly high in developing countries (Clinard and Abbott, 1973), but nowhere has the concern for violence been as great as in the United States, with its steadily rising homicide rate. Not only have the number of murders increased, but the nature of the killings has changed as well.

TABLE 1.1

U.S. HOMICIDE RATES PER 100,000 POPULATION BY FIVE-YEAR TIME PERIODS 1935–1975

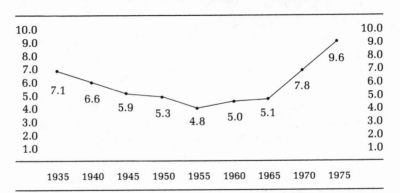

Source: FBI Uniform Crime Reports as shown by Cohn (1976:48)

The rate of homicide for U.S. metropolitan areas increased per 100,000 population from 9.3 in 1965 to 21.3 in 1975 (Block, 1977). For some cities these rates were even higher. The Chicago rate was 25.0 in 1975 (Block, 1977); Detroit was higher yet with a rate of 46.0 per 100,000 by 1972 (Wilt, 1974).

The change in the type of murder that has increased has been noted by Canadian scholars also. A Canadian study indicated that in 1961 personalized types of

TABLE 1.2

MURDER RATES FOR UNITED STATES URBAN AREAS, DETROIT, AND CHICAGO 1940–1975, PER 100,000 POPULATION

Year	U.S.	Urban (Cities 250,000+)	Detroit	Chicago
		Murder Rate		
1940	8.6	5.6	3.9	6.8
1945	5.9	6.5	3.7	6.3
1950	5.1	6.8	4.9	5.9
1955	5.1	6.2	5.2[a]	8.1
1960	5.1	9.5	7.0	10.3
1965	5.1	9.3	9.1	11.5
1970	7.8	17.5	27.3	24.1
1975	9.6	21.3	44.5[b]	25.0
1980[c]	10.4	N.A.	46.0	28.2

Reprinted by permission of the publisher from Richard Block, *Violent Crime: Environment, Interaction, and Death* (Lexington, Mass.: Lexington Books, D. C. Heath and Company, Copyright 1977, D. C. Heath and Company), Table 1-1. Intercensal population was calculated using linear interpolation and in 1975 projection. The Detroit figures were added (Source: Frank E. Hartung and Detroit Homicide Division)

a. 1956 figure
b. 1973 figure
c. 1980 figures. FBI Uniform Crime Reports, 1980 preliminary report.

TABLE 1.3

NUMBER AND RATE OF HOMICIDE OFFENSES IN
CANADA PER 100,000 POPULATION 1961–1980

Year	Number	Rate	Year	wnumber	Rate
1961	233	1.27	1971	473	2.19
1962	265	1.43	1972	520	2.38
1963	245	1.32	1973	546	2.47
1964	253	1.31	1974	600	2.67
1965	277	1.41	1975	701	3.07
1966	250	1.25	1976	668	2.89
1967	338	1.66	1977	707	3.03
1968	375	1.81	1978	658	2.80
1969	391	1.86	1979	631	2.66
1970	467	2.19	1980	593	2.48

Source: Ministry of the Solicitor General, Research and Statistics Development Branch, 1978, 1980

murder were slightly over 50 percent of all homicides; by 1970 this proportion had dropped to about 33 percent (Jaywardene, 1978).

These killings are not what the police refer to as "mommy-daddy" killings or social conflicts between friends and acquaintances. In the U.S. the proportion of all forms of violence towards strangers has increased. The Department of Justice reported in 1973 that in three-fourths of violent crimes the victims were strangers to their assailants (Reid, 1976). Another study showed that by 1972, throughout the U.S., nonprimary and unknown relationship homicides were over 66 percent of the total (Curtis, 1974). The Uniform Crime Reports showed that known or suspected felony homicides had jumped from 17 percent in 1965 to over 27 percent by 1972 (Curtis, 1974) and to 29 percent by 1978.

TABLE 1.4

KNOWN AND SUSPECTED FELONY HOMICIDES IN
THE U.S. 1970–1978, PERCENTAGE OF TOTAL

Year	Percentage
1970	28.8
1971	27.5
1972	27.4
1973	29.0
1974	27.8
1975	32.4
1976	28.0
1977	22.6
1978	29.0

Source: FBI Uniform Crime Reports, 1976–1978 (Washington, D.C.: U.S. Government Printing Office)

RECENT STUDIES ON HOMICIDE

Until recently, there has been a general acceptance on the part of homicide researchers that the majority of murders are the result of interpersonal conflict. Impersonal homicide has been viewed as exceptional, anomalous, and has generated little research. In general, the research on homicide has been primarily confined to statistical analysis or individual case studies. Since 1970, however, there have been several excellent studies focusing on the interactional aspects of homicide. Studies with an interactional focus are those analyzing the symbolic, personal and interpersonal dynamics of the homicide situation as opposed to the longitudinal analysis of individual histories or the statistical analysis of such features as age, sex, or race.

These studies include Richard Block's (1977) work on violent crime in Chicago, containing a comparison of the interactional aspects of homicide with other violent crimes. Included in Block's study of criminal violence are assault, robbery and homicide. He cites death as the outcome of another violent crime as a primary concern. Usually considered felony homicide, this designation also includes death as a result of non-violent crimes such as conspiracy. Block has pointed out that an increasing percentage of the homicides of the early '70s in Chicago stemmed from robberies. He adds that the number of homicides doubled and exhibited a changing pattern (1977:3). Block omits gang and planned killings from his sample and focuses mainly on the victim-killer dyad.

A second study, by Marie Wilt (1974), is on homicide in Detroit. It includes an analysis of felony homicide which she refers to as "crime specific homicide." Wilt compares the social conflict homicide with crime specific and unspecified motive homicides. She presents descriptive statistics and comparisons of the victims and killers on background variables such as race, sex, and occupations. Included are situational, locational, and motivational differences. As Wilt points out, the category of "unspecified homicide" is inaccurate and misleading, as there is sufficient information to classify many of the unspecified homicides (1974:141). She indicates that a large proportion of unspecified homicides are crime related and presents data supporting her views. She also points out that the vast majority (98.2%) of these cases were perpetrator initiated, or performed by persons carrying weapons with them. In many cases, the motive was an apparent gangland killing or it was narcotics related. Indeed, Wilt makes the point that there are really only two types of homicide: social conflict and crime specific, or non-felony and felony as they have been categorized in present research.[2] Both Wilt and Block use statistical analysis to provide useful insights into homicide interactions.

A third study that is concerned with interaction in murder incidents is a descriptive study by Harold Lundsgaarde on homicide in Houston (1977). Lundsgaarde was mainly concerned with non-felony, or what Wilt (1974) refers to as "social conflict murders." He describes the general normative climate that supports the use of violence in homicides. His analysis is thus very similar to others which accept the violent sub-culture hypothesis.[3] Studies by Block (1977), Zimring (1972, 1977), and Fisher (1976) have all clearly indicated the role of a lethal weapon in influencing the outcome of potentially homicidal interactions.[4] However, even the recognition that the use of firearms is likely to increase homicide outcomes is not sufficient to explain the decision to use a gun or another weapon in committing a crime. Nor does it explain the decision to commit murder by persons well aware of the lethality of weapons. We have not been able to assess the influence of familiarity with violence or the presence of a lethal weapon on the expectancy states of killers and victims. Undoubtedly, seeing a weapon will influence the expectations of a victim in a homicide encounter. It will cause the victim to define the situation as more

---

2. Avison (1975:56-58), in a discussion of intent and motive, also points out that homicides have two basic divisions: those that can be seen as primarily problem-solving actions, and those having a more complicated interaction between victim and offender. Levi (1975) contends that all homicides are a form of conflict resolution, even those involving stranger killings.

3. The violent sub-culture hypothesis was advanced by Wolfgang and Ferracuti (1967). While it provides a framework for understanding violence-approving groups, it does not focus on situation–defining or other interactional processes.

4. Skogan (1978:64) defines lethality as "the ability of the wielder of a weapon to inflict grievous harm or death more or less irrespectively of his or her personal attributes (size, weight, skill)." Guns have been shown to be more lethal than other weapons.

dangerous and thus to act in accordance with the outcomes expected in the situation. However, we do not
really know why some of these situations result in
murder while similar situations do not.

All of these studies above recognize the importance of
the homicide situation and how it is defined by the
participants. They all accept, as do most researchers on
homicide, the general absence of pathology on the part
of the participants. Block and Lundsgaarde, in particular, stress that they find little difference between assaul-
tive and homicidal interactions except in the seriousness
of the outcome. Block differentiates the use of force in
robbery homicides as instrumental rather than expressive; Lundsgaarde indicates that lack of concern for the
victim characterizes stranger homicides. Much of the
homicide research emphasizes the importance of the
weapon used in determining whether death or injury is
the final outcome of the interaction. The general data on
homicide as well as these studies give us a number of
general findings regarding age, sex, race, and the like.
Men predominate as offenders and victims, both offenders and victims are relatively young, and the crimes
are usually intraracial (Curtis, 1974).

Some Assumptions About Felony Homicide

1. Homicide and assault are seen as being similar to
   each other while robbery is a different type of crime.
   Interpersonal or social conflict homicide does re-
   semble assault. I believe, however, that felony homicide is more similar to robbery. The question of intent to kill as opposed to intent to rob is problematic
   in many of these cases. First-degree murder is defined as killing with malice aforethought, while
   second-degree murder requires only malice. While

in the acts of contract killing and in robbery itself, we can assume a criminal motive, the intent to kill prior to the encounter is only clear in executions. (It is my contention, however, that killing in a robbery is (a) pre-considered and (b) motivated primarily by self concerns and criminal intent rather than by personal feelings toward the victim. Personal feelings prevail in altercations that result in interpersonal homicide.)

2. The role of strangers in homicides appears to be increasing as are homicides by multiple offenders. The implication is that felony homicide is not the end of a prolonged relationship, but rather has the characteristics of an encounter between several people. Such homicides confirm the need to examine carefully their interactional components and to focus on them as multiperson encounters. *Encounters,* as defined by Goffman (1961), are interactions that continually occur in which people depend on observable characteristics and attribution of roles and traits that will allow them to predict behavior and interact with minimal knowledge about the other.

3. Persons other than the victims and perpetrators are often present. In fact, others were present in 65 percent of the Detroit cases analyzed by Wilt (1974:163).

4. Unsolved murders have increased, indicating the greater possibility of strangers' involvement. There is also a lack of a history of past difficulties to provide clues to police. Although homicide still has the highest clearance rate of serious crimes, its rate has been steadily decreasing, primarily due to the greater difficulty in solving crimes that do not result from prolonged or public conflicts. Felony murderers are likely to select situations more carefully, are less

likely to be known, less likely to confess and more likely to intimidate potential witnesses.

5. Block (1977) and Curtis (1974), both of whom are concerned with crime-related violence, see homicides as largely unplanned. Designating the homicide as unplanned does not necessarily mean that the act of killing or killing under particular circumstances has not been considered; that is, this does not mean that the homicide is impulsive or personal. In Chicago, Block indicates, robbery homicides have increased at a much faster rate than other murders with a known motive. Reed, Blyzinski and Gaucher (1978) point to the increase in gang related homicides in Canada. The Detroit Police Department listed 90 homicide cases in 1974 that were known to be narcotics related. Each of these cases tends to be more instrumental than expressive. In some types, such as robbery homicide, the decision to kill may be considered and confirmed under specific conditions, i.e., if the victims resist or know the defendants. In others it may be postponed and made at the scene.

6. In all recent homicide studies, beginning with Wolfgang's Philadelphia study in 1958, there appear to be large proportions of the defendants having criminal records. A Washington study cited by Robert Sherill (1975:29) showed 62 percent of gun murder defendants having prior records for violent crimes. Wilt (1974) found in the 1972 Detroit homicides that over half of the defendants had prior criminal records.

What all these studies seem to indicate is that we can no longer assume that impersonal, predatory, pre-considered murder is an insignificant part of the homicide picture. These findings indicate that robbery-murder, contract killings and others in the felony homicide category are a different type of homicide from social conflict killings and as such need more thorough and careful consideration. These studies confirm the growing importance of this kind of crime and the need for understanding interactional aspects of felony homicides. Multiple offenders and persons present at but not a party to the homicide are found with increasing frequency. These cases indicate that the focus on the homicide dyad is not realistic in the analysis of felony homicide.

PLAN OF THE BOOK

The plan of this book is to examine the relationship between violence and murder—felony murder in particular in chapter 2. Chapter 3 discusses the data base and methodology used in the study. Part 2, chapters 4, 5 and 6, focuses in detail on three kinds of felony homicides—robbery, execution and sex killings. Part 3 explores the interactional aspect of felony murder, with chapter 7 looking at characteristic behavior patterns. Chapter 8 describes killer styles and career contingencies. Chapter 9 provides a summary of findings and suggests further research.

2 Violence and Homicide: A Conceptual Overview

Violence is defined by the American Heritage Dictionary (Houghton Mifflin) as "physical force exerted for the purpose of violating, damaging or abusing." The variations in the degrees and types of violence in different societies lead us to accept the idea that the majority of violence is learned, rather than innate, and subject to cognitive control rather than being automatic or instinctive. Certain groups and people of certain statuses use violence to a much greater extent than others. Criminal groups use violence as a tool of their trade as do boxers, football and hockey players, police officers, and soldiers. The legitimate use of violence, including killing, is greatly restricted and highly ritualized in modern societies. Legitimate targets for violence have been reduced and there is a tendency in many societies to increasingly criminalize the use of violence even in nonfelony situations. In Sweden, for example, a recent law restricts spanking of offspring by their parents. What appears to be happening is the development of two parallel trends. One is toward the criminalization of interpersonal violence and an attempt to eradicate the use of violence as a a means of resolving interpersonal conflicts. A second trend is the increased use of violence, particularly lethal violence, in impersonal, criminal confrontations.

SUBCULTURAL SUPPORTS FOR VIOLENCE

Subculture refers to an identifiable segment of society that is a part of the total culture but discernibly different in areas such as language or values. There appear to be three major subcultural groups in most westernized societies that provide pro-violence values. These are, first, class-based, primarily lower class, subcultures that support traditional male sex roles and the use of physical violence for control, punishment and prestige.

The second group are the licit occupational subcultures that legitimize the use of violence in occupational contexts under specified conditions. Most important here are the branches of the government that allow violence to be carried to the extreme of killing. The third major subculture is the criminal subculture itself which supports and encourages the use of violence including killing.

THE CHARACTER OF VIOLENT CONDUCT

In some eariler research the character of street violence was elaborated (Dietz, 1968, 1978). The actor learns to recognize cues and becomes ready to use violence in a variety of situations. Most groups do not tolerate members who are unable to restrict their use of violence to targets primarily outside of the group. Even people who are skillful in using violence are not welcome if they are unwilling to control themselves. Thus, by the time a male child in a violent subculture reaches puberty, he has learned that violence is required in some situations and is approved and disapproved in other situations. It can be and is used to control people and to get social rewards and punishments. The violent individual who emerges with street experience—willingly undertaken or not—is one who (1) has learned how to use violence successfully in a variety of situations; (2) frequently does not achieve goals when using other alternatives; (3) has decided that the negative consequences resulting from violence (being feared by others, physical danger and/or pain, possible legal sanctions, etc.) are less than the rewards.

The point should be made that the use of violence is not easy. It requires both physical and mental training. Most of us cannot be violent because we are trained to consider too many issues, to take too long to think before we act. The person who successfully uses violence learns and adheres to these rules:

STREET VIOLENCE NORMS

Be first   Strike first and without warning; conceal your intentions.

Be fast   Hit as quickly and as hard as possible the first time. Do not wait to find out your victim's intentions. The more you hurt him initially the less likely he will be to hurt you. Don't hesitate.

Be final   Get the victim off his feet and immobilize him. Make sure he hasn't the inclination or the ability to get back at you. Kick him when he's down. If you don't put him at least temporarily out of commission, he's likely to come back not only angry but dangerous.

Be careful Keep the odds in your favor. Stay in your own territory. Don't relax and get caught off

> guard. Keep your back to the wall. Locate
> the exits. Don't run your mouth. (Dietz,
> 1968:71–72).

A similar description of these norms appears in the
biography of the Kray twins, well-known criminals in
London, England.

> But from the start they made it clear that they intended
> to become professionals of violence. They had their fan-
> tasies, their jokes, but behind these was one thing they
> took seriously—fighting. Here they knew their job, took
> no unnecessary risks and carefully refused to hamper
> themselves by effete conventions of fair play. These were
> for amateurs. If it was necessary to hit someone, they hit
> first and hardest and put the boot in afterwards. (Pear-
> son, 1972:11)

READINESS TO PERCEIVE VIOLENCE

The continued use of and association with violence in-
creases violence readiness and awareness. Readiness includes having a perception of violence cues, having a
knowledge of and experience with violence skills, and
having cognitive considerations that provide rationalizations for using violence. One cannot have awareness or
cognitive considerations on the spot in a violent encounter because there isn't time. One must be ready to
use violence without having to stop and consider. In
cases of planned violence, some criminals not only use
rationalizations beforehand but also go through a
psyching-up process like that of boxers and pro football players. One Mafia "leg-buster" described it this
way:

> When I have to go out and hurt some guy who
> hasn't paid up I might even like the guy. Then I

think to myself, if this guy did what he was supposed to do, I wouldn't have to go out there. Now I
have to take a chance on getting hurt or getting
arrested and it's all his fault. He knows the rules.
And he's gonna beg and cry and make me feel like
a rat. The dirty fuck. Why is he doing this to me.
I've always been straight with him. I ought to break
his head. Anyhow, by the time I have to go I'm so
mad at the sucker for putting me in this position
that I walk up to him and knock him across the
room. (Field notes, 1973).

EXPECTATIONS THAT VIOLENCE BE CONTROLLED AND DIRECTED ONLY AT SPECIFIED TARGETS

In all pro-violence subcultures, it becomes readily apparent that approval for the use of violence is only available
if the violent actions conform to specified conditions of
purpose, setting, or target. Expressive violence is evaluated by different standards from instrumental violence.
Thus in a boxing match or football game the violence that
is done to an opponent is not supposed to express the
feelings of the actor. If feelings are expressed, they are
expected to have been aroused as a result of some act of
the victim that is interpreted by the actor as appropriate
for arousing those feelings. The same is true in police or
armed services actions. The feeling response is allowed
but only if the person inflicting violence is perceived as
maintaining emotional control.

GENERALLY ACCEPTED JUSTIFICATIONS FOR THE USE OF VIOLENCE

The generally accepted rule for the use of violence, including killing, is that it is justifiable if violent persons
are protecting themselves or their property from viola-

tion by others. This justification is recognized by law. It extends even to persons who are known criminals, if they can prove that they have been attacked without provocation. Using violence is also recognized as necessary in extreme cases to control others and prevent them from committing violence themselves. In the case of control, however, it is rarely seen as necessary to use violence to the extreme of killing. This privilege is usually reserved for police action. In violent subcultures, justification for the use of violence in protecting reputations or self-esteem or for punishing attackers is also available. These are more or less reserved for defensive situations.

The task of handling the protection of body, property and reputation has traditionally been allocated to men. In North American society, generally, this function has been transferred to the police and the law courts or to security guards. Some segments of society have not committed themselves to allowing violent punishments and controls to be turned over to legal authorities. In some areas there has been general dissatisfaction with the handling of violence by the authorities, and these tasks have gradually returned to the citizen. Recent research in Canada, for example, has shown that there is a gradual increase in justifiable homicides by citizens in protection of their homes or businesses (Reed, Blyzinski, Gaucher, 1978). Some groups still maintain the belief that personal assaults, either physical or verbal, should be handled by the injured party because the punishment of the courts is either nonexistent or insufficient.

EXPRESSIVE VS. INSTRUMENTAL VIOLENCE

One distinction that is helpful in understanding felony homicides is the distinction between expressive and instrumental violence. In expressive violence the individual may be seen as having difficulty with control, or at least in appraising the situation or the proper amount of violence to use. In instrumental violence, the person is seen as being in complete control. Members of the actor's peer group must decide if the individual is expressing violence, which is not in his control, or using it instrumentally. Because of the use of the "psyching up" or "berserker" tactics by some users of violence, it becomes difficult to make distinctions at times. There is also a difference in being able and being willing to control violence. The individual's judgment comes into question and it must be determined whether or not that judgment is good given the specific situation.

One way to separate psuedo-expressive violence from truly expressive violence would be to look at the target. At first it would seem that truly expressive violence would be directed at a specific target. The use of rage in crime-motivated violence would be secondary to the crime and the target would be unimportant. In a sense, the latter denies the meaning of expressive violence. Perhaps we can consider the violence instrumental if its aim is other than a response to the target as an individual.

THE WILLINGNESS TO KILL

A major question that must concern us here is whether or not a person is willing and able to kill. Some people do not kill because they believe killing is wrong. Other people do not kill because the circumstances under which killing is acceptable to them do not arise, i.e., defense of home and family. Still others do not kill because of fear. They are afraid they cannot accomplish the act and will be hurt, or they fear the legal consequences. There are people, even those in violent occupations such as police work and soldiering, who have opportunities to kill and who avoid them. There are also such people in the violent subculture. There are many criminals who do not kill when the opportunity presents itself. Even in situations where killing seems most logical—situations in which one killing has already taken place and there are live witnesses—they do not kill matter-of-factly. What we must conclude is that there are a number of people who would kill if the right opportunity presented itself but that there are a number of people who, although trained in violence, are unable or unwilling to kill. The Kray twins again provide an example. Both loved violence.

> Reggie developed what was known as his cigarette punch. With his right hand he would offer someone a cigarette and as the man opened his mouth to take it, would hit him on the side of the jaw with a swift left. It required timing and you needed to know the exact spot to hit. Reggie practiced it for hours on a punch bag and the cigarette punch broke many jaws. An open jaw will fracture easily. (Pearson, 1972:11)

But in spite of Reggie's commitment, experience, and skill with using violence, he would not kill. Ronnie killed and tried continually to persuade or humiliate his twin into murdering too. Although they were very close, Reggie could not go through with it.

> Ronnie never understood the ordinary person's ambivalence over murder. Most people seemed fascinated by it but never dream of doing it; he dreamed of little else. (Pearson, 1972:168)

While learning about violence is likely to provide greater preparation and opportunity for killing, at least for felony murders, there is more involved than just violence training and the opportunity and acceptance of violence values. In his autobiography, self-proclaimed hit man Joey explains it like this:

> ... the majority of the people who make their living in crime ... don't want to hurt anybody. There are a lot of people in the mob who will not pull the trigger, who will not break legs, who will not swing a pipe because they just don't have it in them. I mean, they're larceny-hearted, they're not violent. But the only people who get to the top, as far as making good money, are the people who don't give a fuck, people who would just as soon blow your brains out as look at you, break your leg if it's a necessity, if you deserve it. (Fisher, 1973:19)

THE SELF AND INTERPRETATIONS OF SITUATIONS AS REQUIRING VIOLENT ACTIONS

Lonnie Athens, in his study *Violent Criminal Acts and Actors* (1980), examined the self-concept and mental processes of people using violence. Athens paid particular attention to the way in which the self-concept interacts with the definition of situations leading to violent acts on the part of the actor. He developed a typology of situational definitions that takes into account defensive, frustrative, and what he calls malefic interpretations. Much of the initial stages of any violent encounter involves the process of assessment and attribution of characteristics and intent by actors of each other. As Goffman (1959) has pointed out, in order for an interaction to occur and for the actors to present a particular identity to others, they must be able to make some judgments about the others' characteristics and to develop some expectations of the others' behavior. Athens (1980) has emphasized that the actors who hold nonviolent self-images are able to define situations as requiring violent requiring violent actions only if they see them as dangerous and are able to interpret them defensively. However, when actors hold violent self-images they are able to interpret situations in a variety of ways that permit them to justify the use of violence.

THE EXTENSION OF JUSTIFICATIONS FOR VIOLENCE TO INSTRUMENTAL USE IN FELONY HOMICIDES

A number of writers have examined the way in which criminal acts can be rationalized in order that the actor does not have to damage his self-esteem or confront the inhumanity of his actions. (Hartung, 1965; Sykes and Matza, 1967). However, killing, except defensively, is among the most difficult behaviors to justify. In robbery homicide cases, it is possible to postpone the decision to kill or make it conditional upon some threat to the self or other members of the group. Some robbery groups support use of the threat of violence but restrict approval for killing to situations in which the victim has made a violent move toward them, such as producing a weapon.

DEFENSIVE RATIONALIZATIONS

In defensive rationalizations, a direct defensive interpretation of the situation is made. Group responsibility for the life-threatening situation is disregarded. The actor then kills to defend self or companions but (in his or her own interpretation) not for profit. Defensive rationalizations for killing also are made occasionally in contract situations. They are rare, however, and usually involve the killing of persons who are outside the target.

In the following case we can see how a defensive rationalization was developed by Anthony, who agreed to bring the victim to the killer but who had stated that he was unwilling to take part in the actual killing.

> *I was supposed to get the guy and bring him to Henry. I told him I wouldn't kill him though. He said, "That's O.K. as long as you bring him to me so I can take care of business." He said he was going to kill the guy and burn the car with him in it. The guy was supposed to buy my car so I said, "Let's go and try it out." He started the car and I pulled my gun and said, "Somebody wants to talk to you and it don't make no difference to me either way. I don't want to hurt you, man, just drive on and I'll show you where to go." He said, "Who, man?" I said, "You'll see when you get there. Just drive on, man." I was going around the corner 'cause Henry was following me. I was gonna stop and he was gonna take over and I was gonna take the car that he was driving. Then the guy said, "Hey, what do they want with me, man?" I said, "Hey, as far as I know they just want to talk to you. Don't cause me any trouble cause I don't want to do anything to you. Just go where I tell you." Then he turned the corner, slammed on the brakes and attacked me. The first time the gun went off, but there was three shots so I must have fired two more times. He got out of the car and ran. I stopped the car and started walking. Henry wanted to know how bad was he hurt. I said I didn't know. He said, "It was so close, why didn't you finish him?" I said, "I didn't want to kill him — it was just that he attacked me." It was a different thing then. It was all about me then.*

Anthony was a career criminal who did not want to kill. Even in the situation where he actually shot he became neither angry nor methodical. He was attacked, but he made no attempt to finish the job although he knew he could be identified. He, in effect, deliberately pulled his punches and limited the degree of injury. There are different places at which even hard-core criminals will draw the line. The individual who does not want to kill will attempt to avoid the killing situation.

SECONDARY DEFENSIVE RATIONALIZATIONS

The defensive interpretation can extend to killings in which the decision to kill is justified by the fact that the victim will be dangerous to the killers in the future. This interpretation is made by attributing characteristics of bravery, foolhardiness or vindictiveness to the victim. Based on some act, expression or gesture, either nonverbal or verbal, the killer develops expectations of whether or not this person will seek him out and kill him or testify against him in court. Often, in order to avoid this attribution, victims who know the killers and have witnessed them committing an act of robbery or a murder will issue disclaimers of their interest in seeing the actors punished.

DEPERSONALIZATION/PERSONALIZATION

Depersonalizing occurs in many cases where the victim is known to the killers. They refer to the victim as "the old man" or "the lady" even when they are well aware of the person's name. By dealing with the victim as an impersonal object, they are able to rationalize the killing. The killers are redefining the victim as a barrier to their success. In one case, even though the killer had worked with the two victims for several weeks before the killing, he "forgot" and mixed up their names, although he described several months of planning and the entire murder interaction in minute detail.

Personalization occurs when killers interpret the victim's acts as a personal affront. These killers define the victim as being insulting or disrespectful to them personally. Personalization allows the killers to respond to the victim within the generally accepted norms, permitting violence if there is an attack on the actor's self-esteem. In this way they rationalize that the killing was justified, not in terms of profit, but in terms of their reputations and group expectations.

DOING A PUBLIC SERVICE

Justification for executions and gangland punishments are often facilitated by defining the victim as an evil person who deserves to die. The victim is presented as a person who has violated rules and endangered others or as one who is greedy, unfair or in some other way responsible for bringing his fate on himself. Although the executioner is usually paid for the service, he is able to convince himself that the world is a better place without the victim. Indeed, the public, the press and the police often support this rationalization by emphasizing the past record of the victim.

GLORIFICATION

A final method that killers use to justify their acts is focusing on their definitions of a professional killer or "hit man." The victims in these cases are considered as unimportant, relative to the killer's reputation as a professional or as a "bad dude." By professionalizing the act of killing and emphasizing the skills and management of the murder, the victim takes a secondary position to the killer's identity. The person who is able and willing to kill incorporates the killing into his or her self-concept and is changed. Joey (Fisher, 1979:201) stated, "Within me I know I am playing judge, jury, executioner and God. . . . In a situation like this, you are aware that, for one individual, you are heaven and hell, you are the ultimate."

ROLE-IDENTITY: INCORPORATION OF THE KILLER ROLE INTO THE SELF-CONCEPT

The self is many faceted and in any given setting must be identified both by the actor and by others. Multiple conceptions of the self are mainly derived from roles that can be distinguished as role-identities. For a role identity to become a significant part of the self-concept, a number of stages are normally involved. Horrocks and Jackson (1972) suggest that "each hypothesized identity concept or cluster of identity concepts has to be tested against reality through available social roles."

Hypothesized identities are amenable to modification and are changed as reality proves the identity hypothesis to be inappropriate or ill-conceived. Most persons who become involved in felony homicides have already incorporated a criminal role concept into their identity hierarchy. Some have also incorporated violence into their self-concepts. Most criminal groups discuss the question of killing and the actors hypothesize this question as an identity for themselves and their companions. Their evaluations are added to other evaluative criteria regarding killers and killing that had been incorporated earlier. Upon these negotiations they base their answers—whether or not a killer role identity is salient for a homicide encounter. Some people reject the killer role, saying that they couldn't or wouldn't want to kill anyone; other group members see it as acceptable and desirous at the first opportunity. It is likely, however, that the implications of this act in transforming identity are not fully considered.

For the killer identity, it is extremely important how the label is applied by the rest of the world. Certain acts must be engaged in repeatedly before others will accord an actor an identity based on a specialized role performance. No one is considered to be a dancer or an artist without performing the role many times. Even then the self-identity may develop prior to the recognition of that role. However, some acts are considered to be so important that it is possible that from the time it is known others will regard the actor exclusively in terms of that role. So it is with the act of killing. As a result of this act, a person may be seen solely as a killer from then on. In most cases the murderer has not dreamed of and prepared for this role for years, as has the athlete or artist. Although professional killers often focus around a killer identity themselves, persons in sex or robbery homicide groups may be forced to deal with a permanent identity that they did not plan for carefully nor consider fully. I do not mean to suggest that the act itself has not been considered, but that the identity transforming characteristics of playing this role have not been taken fully into account.

The quickness of the killing act, and the speed of the identity transformation that then may dominate the way in which the killer perceives himself and the way he will be perceived by others, is perhaps one of the most unusual aspects of the enactment of a killer role, compared with other major identity-transforming roles. It is the act of murder, rather than the act of killing, that causes this identity transformation. Killing done by a

police officer or soldier does not have the same effect, at
least not to others. The knowledge that one is able to
kill, in itself, must have a profound effect on the person
who possesses it. The reactions of others, and to some
extent the self, are much clearer and more significant
when they are associated with the intentional murder-
ous act, particularly the profit-motivated murder. Although self-defense can sometimes be developed as a
rationalization, in the cases of executions and execution-
style robberies, it is difficult to conceive of the act in
terms other than murder for profit. The absence of commonly acceptable rationalizations undoubtedly secures
the killer identity more readily.

MULTIPERSON ENCOUNTERS

As has been suggested earlier, a large number of homicide interactions are not interactions of dyads but rather
are multiperson encounters. Although the group has been
considered as important in socialization, most writers
have paid little attention to the group dynamics of violent
encounters. As McCall and Simmons (1978:58–59) point
out, "When there are more than three or four persons, the
characters and roles assigned to each are depicted even
more sketchily and equivocally. . . .Thus, the more
people who are involved, the more difficult it is to gain
even a rough consensus on identities and roles." However, for social plans of action there must be consensual
meanings. In multiperson interactions the meanings are
seldom agreed upon completely and are rarely identical
for all participants.

Not only are there often two performing groups in
conflict in a homicide interaction, but there are also
witnesses or persons who are attempting to disassociate
with all other persons. They must be regarded as an

audience for the two performing groups. Due to the problems of accomplishing goals, coalitions form and groups often allow one representative to speak or effectively make decisions for either group (McCall and Simmons, 1978). The victim group may or may not be prepared to engage in teamwork to the same extent as the homicide group. Often there is little time to negotiate the statuses within the group.

THE DYNAMICS OF VIOLENT CONFRONTATIONS

The dynamics of violent confrontations (Dietz, 1968) can be more easily understood if the confrontations are considered in progressive stages. In this way, we can distinguish between the dynamics of violence that develop in conflictual interpersonal interaction and the violence that is a result of prior planning in criminal cases. Of course, in actual encounters the division into discrete stages is more difficult. Some violent criminal acts are minimally planned, and some progress in stages into violent encounters as a result of confrontations with the victims. The latter is similar to interpersonal violence encounters. For the most part a major difference exists in these two types of violent encounters. The violent criminal act usually begins before the targets are present, while the interpersonal violence encounter begins with both parties or groups present at the initiation and decision-making stages. Violent encounters can be described as occurring in a four-stage sequence. These encounters consist of an initiating act or confrontation stage; a decision to act or negotiation stage; an action stage; and a control stage.

The criminal violence sequence involves stages both before and after the violent encounter when the target is not present. Although the action of the target influences

FIGURE 2.1
STAGES IN HOMICIDE ENCOUNTER

Interpersonal Violence* (Social Conflict Homicide)	Criminal Violence (Felony Homicide)
Initiating Confrontation	Planning Decision
Decision Negotiation	Confrontation
Action	Victim Response
Control	Action
	Escape
	Post- Crime Activities

*Luckenbill (1977) describes five stages in non-felony murder showing both victim and offender decision-making as discrete stages.

the course of the interaction in both types of encounters, it is likely to be much more influential in the interpersonal-conflict-type encounters than in the criminal violence encounters. In the former, a commitment to carry out the crime has been made prior to the confrontation with the target. It is interesting to note that Joey, the contract killer mentioned earlier who described his professional activities in several books, has used similar terms to describe the stages of the contract hit. In a detailed account of one of his contract murder involvements, he makes reference to these stages. He does not divide the stages at exactly the same points as was described above. In his account he had been describing the procedures of following his intended victim for several days in order to determine his schedule. At this point he has decided on a time and location for the hit.

> With the burning of the notes the planning stage ended and the action phases begin. On every hit up until this point, there is always something hazy, something unreal about it. (Fisher, 1975:152)

After the hit, he also describes a stage, which he does not label, that includes getting rid of the evidence. In the particular case that he was describing, it also included his being arrested for suspicion.

In cases of a planned execution then, the stage at which the killer encounters the victim may involve little interaction beyond the actual murder. But there may be a number of prolonged interactions between the killer and other persons involved at some stage of the homicide. In cases in which criminal violence has been planned and the decision has been made, the action, though intended, may be aborted. Interruption or some other reason can cause the postponement. In these intended encounters, the target is not aware of what is going to occur, but it is very much a part of the thinking of the perpetrator. So we can envision a number of interactions in criminal violence cases where a decision has been made concerning the life of the target and of which the target has no knowledge.

In interpersonal conflict violence, on the other hand, both parties often make decisions that will permanently change their lives. Often they have had very little time to consider consequences or alternatives. A required aspect of managing a criminal violence encounter is making the victim sufficiently aware of potential danger to cooperate, but not to believe that death is a foregone conclusion. In the latter case, the victim feels that nothing will be lost by attempting to escape or by attacking. Letkeman (1973), Einstadter (1969) and Shover (1973) all deal with this manipulation of possible danger by the armed robber. So do two of the contract killers discussed in later chapters. Letkeman (1973) has pointed out the importance of social skills and the manipulation of persons in social settings as essential for the career robber. He considers the reinterpreting of features of social settings and the ability to assess risk as part of the robber's necessary skills. Criminals are aware of the problems of managing the encounter and often make reference to the methods that they use. Joey, in the case discussed earlier, mentioned that at one point he thought he knew when the intended victim became aware of his intention to kill him.

> He looked at me and then looked straight ahead. I think that at that moment, for one brief second, just an instant in time, he knew. Then he denied it to himself. (Fisher, 1975:223)

This statement conveys Joey's knowledge of his intended victim's thinking, and brings up the denial of awareness on the victim's part. It is not rare for killers who discuss their cases to interpret their victims' behavior. The killers provide each other with insight into the cognitive processes and decision making that go on during the encounter for the victims and killers alike. In all violent encounters the actors are aware of the dynamics of the participants. Other factors that must be considered are the degree to which the control of the situation is centralized or diffused; the degree to which those in power in the situation are committed to engaging in or preventing violence; and the degree to which the situation is free from external interruptions that may redistribute power or change the perceptions of the participants. Thus, the advancement of potentially violent encounters in the action stage is influenced both by the dynamics between the participants and by external influences on the situation.

SUMMARY

Chapter 2 has provided a symbolic interactionist framework for examining felony homicide as a dynamic, multiperson encounter. The perspective of symbolic interactionism assumes that acts are considered, evaluated, reinterpreted, and modified in a dynamic, neverending process. As interaction occurs, others respond, and their responses are taken into account. Subcultural supports and learning about violence are related to the cognitive processes used to define homicide and rationalize killing. The development of a self-concept amenable to incorporation of the killer role was explored. A model was provided to differentiate the stages of felony homicide from social conflict homicides.

3 The Data Base

Data for this study were gathered through the cooperation of the Detroit Police Department, particularly the Homicide Division. Accounts are analyzed qualitatively to provide an understanding of the types and processes of felony homicide.

The presentation of statistical data is limited, as several excellent sources of statistical data on Detroit homicides exist (Wilt, 1974; Boudouris, 1974; Fisher, 1976; Harris, 1976; Wilt and Bannon, 1974).

The data consist mainly of homicide accounts given by defendants, witnesses, and in some cases, intended victims, or victims who did not die immediately. There were 801 homicide files for 1974. They included the actual statements, autopsy reports, suspect records and a variety of other documents. All of these files were read and classified as felony or nonfelony. Summary records of the 1971 through 1977 homicide files were read. Fourteen hundred fifty-six of these were recorded. Entire files for those cases involving execution and execution-style homicides were read. Cases were designated as felony homicides if they included robbery or the appear-

ance of robbery, rape or sexual molestation, or if they
were an apparent execution or were drug related.

The Detroit Police Department statistics list only one
motive for each case. In some cases they may not designate motives or they may include them as "others" or
unknown. In 1974 they listed under motives: robbery,
179; sex, 14; argument, 310; other, 112; and unknown,
180. They listed separately narcotics involvement in 90
cases. Additional information was found on some cases
after the motive had been designated on the records, but
the initially listed motive was retained in the statistics.
When several crimes occurred together in one homicide
(e.g. rape, robbery, and an argument over narcotics) an
arbitrary single motive was assigned. Thus the designation system used by the police for motive or type of
homicide was not suitable for this study.

Examples are drawn from all these cases as well as
from interviews. I gained knowledge of homicide investigation procedures and additional information on specific cases that were not included in the files through
discussion of cases with homicide detectives during
eight months of work at the homicide division. During
this time I was able to observe crime scenes, autopsies,
and interrogations of witnesses and suspects and to follow several cases through each stage of investigation. I
also conducted and sat in on a number of interviews
with men who were involved in murder for profit. I
conducted lengthy interviews with two men, David and
Ricardo, whom the homicide detectives considered to be
prototypes of robbery and contract killers. It was interesting to find that in many of the later cases, persons
who had been interviewed as witnesses in earlier cases
appeared as defendants or victims. Defendants in earlier
cases also appeared as defendants or victims in later

cases. Both of the people who were interviewed in depth and whose responses are discussed in the book were released and rearrested on new cases involving similar crimes.

A METHODOLOGICAL NOTE

Even if the researcher is so inclined, making field observations of homicide encounters, such as those described in this book, is not a realistic endeavor. In earlier research on violence (Dietz, 1968), I conducted field observations on many incidents of interpersonal violence. Some of these were severe enough to require hospitalization for the persons involved. None of these observations resulted in the death of any of the participants. There are a few other studies of violence that have been based, at least in part, on methods in which the researcher observed the actual incidents of violence. (Prus, 1978; Polsky, 1972; Athens, 1979, 1980.) None of the observations are of homicides. In fact, it is doubtful that, given the opportunity to observe criminal violence, any researcher would be willing to do so. The moral and legal problems that would arise, as well as the danger to the researcher, are prohibitive. Hunter Thompson (1966), a journalist engaged in this type of observation with the Hell's Angels motorcycle club, ended his observations in the hospital as a result of a beating from his subjects.

The above considerations limit the possibilities for firsthand accounts of homicide encounters to interviews with informants. As the victims in these cases are inaccessible, the most common type of interview is with the convicted killer. One rare exception is the interview with a non-convicted killer as reported in the work of Joey with Dave Fisher (1973, 1975). The police files,

which include statements of intended victims, witnesses, and deathbed statements by victims, as well as
statements by suspects, offer the widest range of eye-
witness accounts of homicides.

As this type of account, in addition to the two interviews with non-convicted killers, has been selected for
this study, there are several questions that might be
raised with regard to the validity of the data. The questions involve, first, the truthfulness of accounts that are
given under these circumstances and, second, the cap-
ability and possible bias of the persons taking the accounts. With regard to the former there is the problem of
how accurate the account is of any interaction involving
an informant (Becker, 1970). The accuracy is difficult to
judge as there is evidence indicating that all accounts
are distorted and that this is even more true when extreme emotion is involved on the part of the observer
(Douglas, 1976). We must recognize and acknowledge
then that there is distortion. Distortion of facts is also
common in criminal cases such as rape or robbery and
must be considered as part of the nature of the data.

In addition, the very circumstance of being interviewed in relation to a murder case, whether it is a
felony murder or social conflict, creates additional ten-
sion for the respondent. There is fear, even for the innocent, that they will be considered responsible in some
way for the murder.

There is also a tendency for the persons interviewed to
present their account in a way that the police describe as
self-serving. That is, they describe their own involvement so as to cast themselves in the best possible light.
The self-serving type of distortion may not be only in
regard to the homicide, but also to conceal any other
illegal activity that may be found out. While this is a

common tendency, it is maximized in the accounts given in homicide cases. Being regarded as a potential witness, as well as suspect, is something to be feared by the respondent. On a more positive note with regard to truthfulness, many accounts are compared to others and discrepancies are noted and investigated. Finally, most accounts have to be repeated a number of times, making false statements more difficult to maintain.

In the second problem area, we can consider more carefully the skills and the procedures of the homicide detectives. First, the homicide detectives are experienced in handling the reports of crime before they ever move to the homicide division. With rare exceptions, the entire division consists of persons who are at the rank of sergeant or lieutenant. Second, homicide detectives spend a substantial amount of time conducting interviews. Third, they almost always work in pairs or groups so that each important statement has the benefit of being examined by two or more persons. Fourth, they are very sensitive to discrepancies and deception. It is true that some detectives are more effective at eliciting information than others, a fact that they themselves recognize. They are all interested in solving the cases and are willing to ask for help from the other members of the division.

My own evaluation of the quality of the data, having read hundreds of accounts of all types of homicide cases, is that the end result is as accurate an account of the encounter as one will get, considering the subject. Some cases are extremely sketchy, and others have a wealth of detail. The statements of some suspects are audio or video recorded and transcribed, while others are terse statements taken in longhand or written by the suspect. For the researcher, the recorded and transcribed statements of all persons interviewed would be ideal, but the logistics of such recordings for homicides in a metropolitan area are unrealistic.

In summary, then, I believe that given the amount of data, a reasonably accurate picture of felony homicides will emerge. The names of the killers and victims in this study have been changed to preserve the confidentiality of the police files and interviews. However, the majority of these cases have been reported in the media and many have been tried in court. Therefore, they are a matter of public record. An effort was made to preserve the feeling of the accounts by substituting similar types of names or nicknames.

PART TWO

The second section of this book examines, in more detail, three major types of felony homicide: robbery homicide, executions, and sex killings. Accounts from felony homicide case files and interviews are used to describe and differentiate the tasks and social organization of these killings. As has been emphasized before, the designation of felony homicide indicates that the killing is crime related. The majority of the killers are people who have already embarked on a criminal career. There are differences, however, in the motivation and intent in the three types of murder. There are differences also in degree of planning and group involvement.

4 Robbery Homicide: Your Money and Your Life

Robbery homicide is difficult to categorize, as is robbery itself. On the one hand, it is a personal crime involving a confrontation with the victim, and on the other, it is a theft involving the taking of money or property. Robbery, even without homicide, is a violent crime, involving injury, threat of injury, or death for the victim. It is also, as Block (1977) has pointed out, the most rapidly increasing form of homicide.

MOTIVATION AND INTENT

Intent to kill has created problems for legislators in attempting to work out penalties for armed robberies and other combined crimes. Many lawmakers contend that the act of carrying a weapon to a crime scene is tantamount to admission of intent to use it in committing the crime.

In sociopsychological terms, motive and intent are different concepts. In court, motivation is sometimes used by the prosecution to prove intention. Basically, motive is broad and general. It refers to the emotion, desire, or need that incites a person to action. Any given

motive may result in haphazard action in mány directions. Intent, however, is narrow and specific. It refers to
a purpose or goal that a person has in mind. It is what
the person wants to happen. From this it would seem
that although the motive of profit might be the same for
both the robbery and execution killer, the intent in one
case would be to rob and in the other to kill. Unfortu-
nately, it is not that simple. Although the police may
assign a primary motive of robbery in one case and
murder in another, the fact that a robbery occurs does
not mean that the intent to kill was not present. The
intent in both cases is criminal.

In some robbery cases the intent is to rob, and the
killing is the result of a defensive reaction to the specific
situation. In other cases, the intent exists both to rob and
to kill. This is particularly true in cases where the killers
are known to the victim or where the victims are seen as
likely to seek revenge.

TYPES OF CASES INCLUDED

The murders discussed in this section are primarily
those in which it appeared that the primary intention
was the robbery itself, although there are some in which
the decision to kill the victim was made prior to the
encounter. In 1974, in 161 of the murders that occurred
in Detroit that year, a robbery or robbery attempt also
occurred. Seventeen were execution-style robberies.
Those cases in which it appeared that the primary intent
was the execution will be discussed in the following
chapter. The robbery homicide cases discussed here
were selected from cases between 1971 and 1977. Material from interviews and accounts of robberies and robbery killings by David and his group are included in this
chapter. David was twenty-one at the time of the interviews. By the time he was seventeen, he and his group

had been involved in over two hundred robberies and rapes and in six robbery homicides. David's group was in no way atypical of robbery homicide groups.

THE ROBBER

Robbery is defined as the taking of money or other items from a person or persons in face-to-face confrontation, using force or the threat of force. As Einstadter (1969) describes the robber, he thinks of himself as honest and courageous. He sees himself as superior to the con man who gets his money through trickery or the burglar who robs when the victim is not present. In a sense he sees his act as one that gives the victim a chance. It is not an equal chance, however, as we can see from his frequent choice of the old, the weak, or the most vulnerable victim. We must add to this the fact that the victim is often unarmed and one against many. However, when we look at the statistics on private gun ownership and armed security guards, or we observe the frequent robbing of armed dope houses, perhaps in some cases the image of the courageous robber is true (Sherrill, 1973; Ministry of the Solicitor General, 1976).

WEAPONS IN ROBBERIES

Most homicides in North America are done with handguns. The use of handguns in robberies is considered to have increased greatly the odds of critical injury being inflicted during the robbery (Zimring, 1968, 1972; Block, 1977). However, all robbery groups do not carry guns to the scene; some prefer to pick up their weapons on the spot.[1] To some extent this is due to the haphazard or

---

1. Skogan (1978:64) quotes a 1974 study by Repetto, who suggests that house burglars fear being unable to control their own actions. They also fear the consequences of a homicide conviction. Therefore they avoid confrontations that require weapons.

the haphazard or spur of the moment type of planning that goes into many robberies. Given the ready availability of guns and the fact that many people are armed with weapons at all times, not bringing a gun to the scene is likely only the preference of certain groups. As the members of these groups are usually experienced criminals, they know that there are advantages that result from not having taken a weapon to the crime scene if they are caught.

In cases where robbers use fists and feet as weapons, or where they leave victims tied and gagged to suffocate, it is perhaps not so much that they want to kill the victims as that they don't care whether or not the victims die.

ATTITUDES TOWARD THE VICTIMS

Mead has pointed out that taking the role of the other person is an integral part of human interaction. Charon (1979) goes even further, saying that role-taking ability amounts to what might be called social intelligence. A recent extensive study on the criminal personality, however, maintains that this empathy is the very area in which criminals are deficient (Yokelson and Samenow, 1976). How is it that criminals who must be able to take the role of the other person in order to plan and execute their crime can do so without developing an identification with and empathy for their victims? In other words, the robbers must be able to understand and predict their victims' actions without becoming too sympathetic.

In the initial stages of many robberies, particularly house robberies, at least one member of the group must gain admittance and interact with the victims until the others gain admittance and the robbery is announced.

Since there appears to be no deficiency in role-taking abilities either with the victims or in relations with others, there must be another way to account for their ability to understand but not sympathize. I believe they devise a victim relationship requiring that no feeling interfere with the crime. During their initial crimes, those who are not able to be objective and depersonalize victims probably drop out. This depersonalization is very similar to the training surgeons receive that allows them to proceed with operations without allowing their feelings to surface and interfere with their work. Thus, we are suggesting that when criminals begin to interact with victims, they develop a compartmentalization of feelings.

GROUP INVOLVEMENT IN ROBBERY HOMICIDES

As was pointed out, it no longer seems viable to consider homicides as exclusively dyadic interactions. This is particularly true of felony homicides, over half of which involve multiple offenders. Even in interpersonal conflict killings, there are often others present. Small group research has repeatedly confirmed that the presence of others is taken into account by actors when considering actions (Shaw, 1976). When the observation and actions of others is likely to have significant consequences for the action, their influence in the thinking of the actors is even greater. The essential components of many felony homicides consist of group discussion and planning in the pre-encounter phase, interactions between victim(s) and killers during the homicide encounter, and post-encounter interactions.

At each stage the presence of and interaction with others has direct and indirect effects on the homicide encounters.

THE ARMED ROBBERY GROUP

Miller (1978), basing his analysis on the work of Einstadter (1969), DeBaun (1950), Letkeman (1973), and
Shover (1972, 1973), has reviewed the social organization of armed robbery. He points out the necessity of
having a group, rather than an individual, carry off most
robberies, but he also explores the flexibility of the robbers' roles within their group. The division of labor
described in these studies is very similar to that of robbery homicides. Miller emphasized that research on
armed robbery groups has indicated that members have
equal status in the group. David also stressed this fact,
especially in developing plans. However, in the actual
small group situations in which the crime is "going
down," some members have more power than others.
Both the stress that is involved in small group activity
and the crime situation itself influence which of the
group members will assume leadership in the encounter
(Hare, 1976). Certain tasks must be done. In some groups
they are handled in different encounters by the same
people; in others they are not.

In focusing on the group dynamics involved in felony
homicides, it becomes immediately clear that the potential actions and reactions become multiplied and complicated enormously by the addition of even one other
person, let alone several. The group members are much
more easily able to depersonalize situations that involves "us" and "them" than those that involve "me"
and "you." The situation comes to be defined as a power
struggle between two opposing groups. The responses to
actions on the part of victims are reinterpreted in light of
group loyalty which in this type of situation means
group and individual survival. An act of aggression to-

wards victims can be more readily rationalized if the member can define the act as being a service to the group as opposed to self-motivated. Members recognize that their conduct is being evaluated by other group members. There seems to be an understood necessity to maintain the appearance of cohesiveness for the victims. The recognition that disagreements in front of the victims will increase their own vulnerability seems to influence the way group members voice objections to other members' behavior. While members may question each other after the crime is completed as to why they acted in a particular way, they rarely will voice more than a token protest on the scene. There also appears to be a norm of reciprocity that operates, although this reciprocity may have been implied, and not brought out, in any of the accounts. It involves the recognition that group members have individual, as well as group, motives that influence their behavior at the crime scene. The rule appears to be that behavior that is not in direct conflict with the primary group motive will be tolerated. Thus, one member's property destruction, or another member's sexual behavior, will not be objected to strongly.

David, in discussing the dynamics of his group, mentioned a number of occasions in which he voiced half-hearted objections to the behavior of other members. There were times when he had mental reservations and did not voice objections at all. He also discussed the different relationships among the group members and how this influenced their behavior on the scene. He pointed out, for example, that Dwayne would do anything Donald wanted him to but that he himself would only go along with Donald's wishes if they suited his own purposes. He further said that he would not intervene in the acts of Donald or Dwayne, although he did not always approve of them. This unstated agreement, not to intervene among the crime group members, is important in the robbery situations in which sexual assaults or homicides occur. The members having equal status in these groups do not intervene unless they can relate such intervention to the need for safety or success of the group.

In most of the examples cited, there are group situations and group involvement both in the planning stages and at the murder scene. The group members are aware, at some level, that there is some likelihood of a murder occurring. In some cases the strategy is planned out and discussed in specific detail. In others, the group members have been involved in many other activities, and their cooperation and complicity is taken for granted by the shooter. In many felony murder cases the roles, specific tasks, and degree of involvement in the actual killing has been worked out by the group members ahead of time. Occasionally these change, as in the case of David, who stepped into the "shooter role" on one occasion, but not before or after that time. In continued associations, certain roles may become more identified with certain members, depending on their particular skills and on their desire to establish a specific role identity.

MAJOR TASKS IN ROBBERY HOMICIDE

- *initiating, planning*
- *arranging transportation*
- *gaining entry (often done by women)*
- *initial evaluation of situation*
- *disarming*
- *searching*
- *questioning/torture*

- guarding/restraining
- killing
- driving getaway vehicle
- evaluation of member performances
- dividing loot

As will be seen in the following descriptions of robbery homicides, the planning and execution require teamwork and cooperation. Group members who initiate the robbery and lead the planning discussions are not necessarily the same ones who lead during the homicide encounter. Even the shooter role, which separates the robbery from robbery homicide, may be taken by various members on different occasions.

THE GENERAL PICTURE

A robbery homicide may occur on any night, like other felony homicides and unlike interpersonal conflict homicides, which tend to be more frequent on weekends. It may occur in the street or parking lot, in a place of business or in the victim's home. Over half of all robbery homicides involve two or more perpetrators and most take place in front of witnesses. In many cases, there is more than one robbery victim, although not all of them may become homicide victims. The victim may be killed because of real or fancied resistance, to eliminate possible identification of the robbers, or because one or more of the robbers want to kill.

THE SEQUENCE OF EVENTS

The events involved in felony homicide generally occur in three more or less discrete stages: the planning stage, the homicide encounter, and the post-homicide period.

THE PLANNING STAGE

As has been mentioned earlier, the planning stage in robberies may be exceedingly limited. Einstadter (1967) mentions that this is partly due to the nature of robberies. He points out that outcomes are extremely difficult to predict. In some groups, such as David's, where these activities are a nightly occurrence, there is limited planning. Even in a case in which two dope dealers were kidnapped and killed, the planning was not detailed. Most of the time, according to David, the group met every night after going their own way for social activities and drove around until they spotted a likely victim.

Groups commit a large proportion of robberies. Sometimes the groups have up to six or seven members. Probably most common is the group of three to five. All of the group members may not be together during the planning. In one case, two group members stole a car and then went to see who else wanted to continue the robbery with them. There were seven or eight people altogether and only one car. They decided that if everybody went, it would be too crowded. They narrowed the group down to four people. In most of these robbery groups everyone doesn't have a car, and even when they do, they prefer not to use it. It is customary to steal a car, use it for several days, then abandon it and steal another. Often cars will be borrowed from relatives or friends who are not involved, and if the car is spotted or they think it might cause a problem it is abandoned and the owner is instructed to report it stolen.

The robbery group, then, is not consistent, although one or two of the core members of the group usually participate. A group often will have one person who acts as the initiator, although anyone can make a suggestion.

In many robbery groups the members hang around together and, in their general conversation, consider rip-off possibilities. They may select two or three likely places and then rob the easiest or most feasible first. Sometimes they postpone a job for a better time or a time when they have more information. Different locations or potential victims may be suggested by any group members. They are then discussed and approved or rejected for various reasons. Serendipitous information that a member picks up on someone having a large amount of money often helps to select a target.

David describes the planning of robberies in his group.

I started doing serious crimes (more than shoplifting) when I was around 12 years old, with Donald, Dwayne, Albert and LeRoy. I knew them from around the neighborhood. My mother did try to keep me straight but I just wasn't interested. But my folks knew I was stealing, they had to 'cause I always had money and stuff and I wasn't working. I always knew what I was doing right from the beginning, I mean, I knew right from wrong. Most of our crimes weren't planned. Like I'd go out and party or go to the show or to a bar. Then around 2 o'clock we'd sort of drift together. Sometimes I'd look for them or else they'd come and find me, stop by my house or call me on the phone. Donald was the idea man. He's smart. He talks good and he can manipulate people. Sometimes, like Donald had a lot of associations with drug people—he would meet someone and plan to rip them off. Dwayne was a quiet guy and he idolized Donald. He hardly ever said anything. But none of us really hung around together. *Like we weren't friends except for the crimes we did together. Those guys never did anything the rest of the time but stay home and watch TV. They didn't have girls, only me and Donald. Like I mostly hung around one of my ladies. I was livin' at three places, with two ladies and at home. None of those guys were friends. Oh, Dwayne probably would have hung around Donald if he would've let him. Donald was like sadistic. Like he was mean, only a lot of times he'd say stuff in a joking way. He was the only one that ever got in fights 'cause he had a big mouth. He usually won too, 'cause he knew how to win. Most people were scared of Donald. I wasn't scared of him but a lot of guys were.*

Most of the stuff we did was no planning to it. Just spur of the moment stuff. Like even though Donald sometimes suggested things, he didn't care how it was done, just as long as it was done. Like sometimes he'd have an idea and one of us would say 'no way we gonna do it like that.' You know, he didn't have to persuade us—we were all ready. Like he never led me into anything. If I wouldn've never met Donald I would have still been doing crimes. I've did crimes by myself. Maybe I might have done some different things but I always knew what I was doing. I had my eyes wide open and I was aware of what was going on all the time. Like we didn't talk much before we did some of those crimes. Lots of times I didn't need the money. It was more like a habit. Like crime is like an addiction, like heroin.

In David's group, Donald was considered to be the leader, although all of the group members had been involved in crimes in which he had no part. Donald intended to move up and become a big man in the crime world. He used the other group members to build his reputation and help him get the necessary money. He only associated with them in crime activities, preferring the established dope men and players and aspiring to their life-style. Donald preferred to organize, give orders and remain in the background after the crime was initiated. He liked to get others to handle the more dangerous or mundane tasks. He was not averse to taking part in the murders, usually pairing with Dwayne or LeRoy, but he was concerned with his own safety. If there were any females among their victims, both David and Dwayne considered rape an essential part of the robbery activities. Donald was usually the driver, as he had access to a car. He supplied the weapons and had the final say on dividing the loot. Dwayne supplied muscle and generally did whatever tasks Donald told him to.

The following are accounts of the planning stage by different members of a robbery homicide group consisting of two women and five men. The group members committed at least seven murders, two of them double homicides. One was a shooting committed by one of the women; another was a double shooting by one of the men. Three of the others, committed by two other men, were a double and single homicide. They were execution style and the victims were tied. The group ranged in age from 19 to 26. Among other crimes, they robbed and killed a dope dealer, their own landlord, and a jewelry store owner.

The accounts of the planning of the following case are what the police label as "self-serving." Each person attempts to show the idea as originating from someone else.

Carrie, one of the two female group members, describes the planning phase of one robbery homicide.

*We—Lamont, Beau, Butch and I—were riding
around. Lamont said, "I know where we could get
up some money." (It was a dope house). Beau said,
"The only problem is getting in there. Willie isn't
gonna let any man inside there. We'll have to try to
get Carrie inside." Lamont thought for a while then
he said, "Let's call Geraldine and ask her if she's
got any ideas. She's been there lots of times, in fact,
she's the one that took me there." Lamont went to a
phone booth and called her. He talked for a while
then he yelled at me, "Hey, Carrie, come on and
talk to Geraldine." Geraldine told me, like, "Hey,
you won't have any problem about getting in there
'cause that dopeman—he let any woman in. Just
mention my name when you're at the door so he'll
know you're o.k." I told her thanks and went back
to the car. I said, "She told me the guy on the door
likes girls and for me to tell him she sent me. So I
can get in o.k., but you know if he doesn't let me in
then I'm not gonna push the issue, I'm just gonna
leave." Beau said, "Don't worry about that 'cause
he's gonna let you in. Now, when you get in you
wait for me to knock on the door. When you hear
me knock you take the pistol out of your purse and
cover the doorman."*

Notice, in this case, the major problem is getting into the
house. The fact that everyone would be willing to commit the crime was taken for granted. Also, other acquaintances could be involved with little fear of their inform-
ing or notifying the police. The questions of who would

get what or what would happen inside was not discussed.

The robbing of dope houses and gambling places is always attractive. There is usually cash and often drugs, and the victims are reluctant to call the police. Most dope pads and gambling games are in private homes or apartments if they are a small operation. The smaller operators live in the pads and the larger operations have a dealer who stays there when the pad is operating. In both cases there is usually someone who is armed and admits only certain people.

Lamont tells of planning another robbery and double homicide.

About a week before, we were sitting around De-dra's apartment; there was me, Darryl, Jordan, Beau and Dedra. We were going to rob a supermarket that day when Carrie came down. She was in her house-coat like she just got out of bed. She and Dedra started talking about paying the rent that day. Dar-ryl said, "The landlord should have lots of money up there." Dedra said, "They shore do. You all should get them then I won't have to pay no rent." Lamont said, "Do they pay in cash or checks?" Dedra said, "It's mostly cash." Jordan said, "That's easier than robbing a supermarket. We don't even leave the building." Beau said, "No, man, leave 'em be. They're old and besides, they know us." Lamont said, "Yeah." Darryl told me, "Do what you want. I'm gonna anyhow. Carrie, go ask them for a key — tell them you lost yours." Carrie said, "No, the manager knows me, why can't Dedra go?" Darryl says, "It don't matter if they know you, they won't be alive anyhow."

In this case there are two things to note. First, Carrie was able to object to her task and, in fact, she did not go but babysat for Dedra's child. Second, all of the group members, in spite of minor objections, agreed to the choice of victims and knew that Darryl intended to kill them.

The intent to kill as well as rob the two victims was known prior to the homicide and was part of the overt planning of the group. Later, some members of the group may have maintained that they were not aware that a murder was intended. Indeed, sometimes they do object or leave and decline to participate. In the above case, they were all aware that they could be identified by the couple.

In the following accounts of planning, Lamont and Carrie describe a double homicide in which Carrie contended that they discussed what would be done with the victims, and Lamont promised that the victims would not be killed. In their accounts, Carrie describes the robbery as Lamont's idea while he attributes it to Carrie.

Carrie's story:

> One night before Thanksgiving, I was sitting in a car with Lamont and Beau. We had all been to a dope house downtown. Lamont said, "We could get a lot of money for that component set. That's JoJo's apartment. They would have some money there. We'll just tie them up and leave them. We won't hurt them."

Lamont's story:

> On the night of the big snow, Beau, Carrie, Beau's girlfriend and myself went riding and we were discussing what we were going to stick up. Carrie mentioned a friend of hers where we could possibly get

*some drugs and some money. So we went over to
John R. Carrie rung the outside doorbell and told
her who she was. She rung the buzzer and let us in.*

In the following case, an acquaintance, who is aware of
the group's activities, asks to become part of the group.
After their initial entry, they postpone the robbery because there are too many people in the house. Then they
return later.

Beau talks of bringing a new member in on a murder.

*Barry asked me, "Take me with you guys to stick
up a dope house." I said, "O.K." Me and Lamont
and Jordan went over on Woodfield. Barry and me
went in the house and bought some dope and went
back to the car. Barry said, "There's five people in
there." Jordan said, "Let's wait—we drive around
for a while." So we came back in two hours.*

In the final case that will be discussed for this group,
Darryl was involved in suggesting the victim. Although
he told the group he would meet them there, he never
showed up. He later told his girlfriend, Dedra, that he
did not go because he knew the victim would be killed
by Lamont and Beau. He did not make any effort to keep
her from going, however. Nor was he reluctant to kill.
He had already been the shooter in three cases the group
was involved in before this one.

Carrie describes the planning.

*About two days after the big snowstorm, I think it
was Tuesday or Wednesday, I was at Lamont's
house. Lamont's father lives there. Beau, Lamont,
Dedra, me, and Darryl was all there. We were all in
Lamont's bedroom. Darryl was telling Lamont that
this lady on Oak had a lot of money and some weed*

*too. Darryl said, "I'm gonna go over there and wait
for you." Lamont said, "We'll meet you there at her
house."*

*Lamont, Beau, Dedra and me got in Lamont's car
and went to Darryl's house. The three of us stayed
in the car while Lamont went in for five minutes.
Then we drove out to Oak Street.*

In the following two cases, the subject of committing
the robbery is brought up, but very little detail is described. In the first case, the reluctant partner is con-
vinced by the initiator, then later a third party is contacted. In the second case, an additional member was
also recruited after the initial idea had been introduced.

*Early Wednesday morning, about 2 a.m., I was over
at my boyfriend's and we were talking about how we
didn't have any money. I told my boyfriend, Wesley,
that I knew a guy that might have some money. I
called Charles and asked, "Hey, what are you doing?" He said, "Nothing." I said, "Well, I'm gonna
come over then." He said, "O.K." I said, "Come on,
Wesley, let's go rip him off." Wesley said, "No, I
really don't think we should." I said, "We've gotta
do something to get some money. Come on, we need
to get some money." Wesley finally said, "O.K., we'll
go borrow my mother's car." After we got the car he
said, "Let's get Perry to go with us." I said, "You
guys, leave so he can't see you then I'll get him to
open the door so you can get in." We parked next to
his car and I told them, "Get out of the car so he
don't see you if he looks out the window."*

In the first case the planners felt that they needed
additional personnel. In the second case, however, it is

likely that the person giving the account was only asked along because they happened to see him on the street and they thought he would be a willing participant.

> I met Guileo, Greg, and Robert on the street. Guileo said, "You want to make some money?" I said, "How?" Guileo said, "There's this old couple that live in a big house on Chicago. They'd be easy to rip off. I made a delivery there so I know the layout." We got in Greg's van. Guileo said, "Go by my house. I think I've got a receipt with the address on it." He came back and told what the address was. The plan was that Guileo would go up to the door with a package. Someone would follow and when the people opened the door both would go in on them and call the other two guys that were waiting in the truck.

As with the robbery-murder plan that was described in Truman Capote's In Cold Blood, the planning stage may extend over several years and travel through a number of groups' changes. The plan may be discussed without any commitment to execution. It may be developed as new information is gained, or new personnel is added to the robbery group. In the majority of the robbery homicide cases examined for this study, the planning time was short and the robbery was usually executed within one or two days.

The length of time does not have much influence on the type of plan developed. The plans are generally loose, with flexible roles. That is, these groups do not have (1) a driver; (2) a break-in person; (3) a questioner; (4) a person to tie up the victims; (5) a shooter; (6) a collector/searcher; (7) a lookout. These task roles are volunteered for or assigned at the time of the robbery, particularly since the groups do not always involve the same persons. Naturally, group members will repeat roles in which they demonstrate proficiency or will avoid or be left out of roles they handle poorly. However, there tends to be little rigidity in role assignments and minimal detail in planning.

This lack of planning is regarded as impulsivity by many researchers. The real consideration, however, is the difficulty in actually anticipating robbery situations sufficiently well to make elaborate planning worthwhile. In any case, frequently a number of people, besides those involved in the actual robbery, know about or are present during discussions of robbery plans. Often friends want information on persons likely to be present; others will be contacted to procure weapons and cars. This is more a commentary on the acceptability of such ventures within the community than directly related to planning. Most of the members of these groups started robbing together, or with similar groups, in pre-teen and early teen years. In David's group, as they grew older, they drifted together each night at bar closing time and then drove around looking for a likely place for a crime. Rarely would David's group make any specific plans. However, they would carry guns or stop to pick up guns they kept at home. They had developed a signal that if someone whistled, they left immediately. After a while, they understood these cues, making decisions during the robbery, rather than anticipating ahead of time.

We tend to look at these activities as unique events, rather than day-to-day occurrences.

The planning stage can be summarized as follows.

1. Plans, such as they are, are usually executed within 48 hours.

2. Robbery-homicides are committed by persons who regularly commit other crimes or robberies without murder. Some robbery groups also do contract killing.
3. Although members of the robbery group may be prepared to murder, the murder is usually agreed upon or understood ahead of time if:
   a. the perpetrators will be recognized—that is, are known to the victims;
   b. reprisals would be expected beyond a usual possibility—as in some dope house, gangland type' robberies;
   c. the robbery is secondary to an execution;
   d. resistance is encountered that endangers the members or may prevent them from getting away.
4. There are usually attempts to have optimum numbers of perpetrators in robbery crimes. There seems to be a preference for four, but the norm is from three to five.
5. While groups do develop preferences for types of targets, such as homes, businesses, bars, etc., most groups do not limit their targets.
6. The presence of weapons, unexpected persons (such as children, visitors) or insignificant rewards, seems to be less important than would be expected.
7. The short planning period, relatively indiscriminate selection of victims, and frequency of robberies make it difficult for the police to catch criminals for specific crimes. The type of crimes being committed and the type of groups committing them are very similar.
8. Very often there is a group member who is the idea person or initiator at this stage. As in other small group activities, group members without someone to fulfill this role have difficulty getting started.

THE HOMICIDE ENCOUNTER

The actual homicide encounter begins with the start of the robbery, usually the entry into the home or building. Robbery homicides do, of course, also occur on the street and in cars. This stage is marked by the interaction between the criminals and the victims. In the majority of robbery homicides, the final decision to kill any or all victims is made at this stage. As was mentioned above, although group members may be prepared to kill, the decision to kill formalized beforehand only in very few cases. Usually there is limited (if any) discussion beforehand about what will be done in case a victim draws a gun, resists, or attacks. In some places, such as in private homes where the victims are tied or easily controlled, there are conferences among some or all of the assailants about what to do with the victims. In other situations, the killing is done without consultation. In some cases, where there is an overt act of resistance, one member will tell another to shoot or will suggest leaving.

The group members consider both the way they are being viewed by the victims and by the other group members. They also try to decide which of the people present are likely to attack or attempt to escape. While most of the group members are aware of what constitutes evidence in court, they tend not to think about being caught or identified. It is a different situation if they are known to the victim.

The following cases are divided into two types: cases in which the victim(s) is immobilized; and cases where the victim is perceived as a threat to a group member or in which the victim makes a move to escape.

The interaction takes place between victims and various group members, and among group members themselves. Usually, during the action phase, the group members are all in a stage of heightened excitement.

Robbery Homicide in which the Victim is Immobilized

The following account is of a robbery and planned double murder. The victims are a female dope dealer and her friend. The killers are a male and female couple who are both addicts. Frankie had been to Phyllis' apartment earlier to ask for drugs on credit. Phyllis refused and Frankie was angry.

> I asked her for $25 worth of dope on credit and she said no. She said someone had ripped her off for ten packs. The lying bitch. I spend hundreds of dollars with her and when I ask for a little credit she says no. I'll bet that's the last time she says no. I'm going to slit her throat.

Dottie, the female defendant, describes the sequence of events.

> Frankie woke me up and said, "Hey, Dottie, come on. We're gonna go up and take Phyllis out for drugs and some money. You gonna get about $400 and a nice mess of drugs." We talked about how to do it and I went and got some scissors and a towel and some pantyhose that I stuck in my pockets. Frankie got a gun and a hammer and put them in his belt. We went upstairs and I knocked on the door. Phyllis answered and said, "Who is it?" I said, "It's me, Dottie." She let me in and I sat down at the table. I said, "Do me a favor. Let me get a half spoon of mixed jive until later?" She said, "No, I can't do that." I waved my gun and told her to get

back in the bedroom and I let Frankie in. Sandy was in the bed asleep and I pulled the gun on her and told her to get up. Then Frankie came back there and he tied them up and gagged them. I put the telephone wire around Phyllis. I laid my gun down then. Phyllis said, "Say, you're not gonna take me out, are you?" Frankie said, "No, we're not. We're just gonna make it look good you know." Sandy asked me, "Leave me a do." And Phyllis asked me, "Leave me a do, too." I said, "Alright." Just like that. Then Frankie hit them on the head. He hit Phyllis first then he hit Sandy. He said, "Bitch, don't scream or make no noise." Then he started cutting Phyllis' throat and she was moaning."

In the above case, the decision to kill during the robbery was very clearly made prior to entry. Both members of the team participated in a number of tasks such as tying and searching, although Dottie, who gave the account, denies actually participating in the killing.

I went into the kitchen because I, you know, I couldn't stand the, you know, the . . . I couldn't stand the horror and the pain and the agony that they were going through. I waited in the kitchen and then Frankie came in and he asked me, "Do you think they're dead? Do you think they're dead?" And I said, "If they aren't after all them stabbings, they will be by the time anybody gets to them," because they were bleeding to death. He said, "Well, where is Phyllis' heart at because I'm not sure she's dead." I said, "It's underneath her left breast." And he asked me, "Come on back and feel her pulse." So then they were both dead and we got $200—no, $150 and about $300 worth of drugs. Then we left out and we got rid of the evidence; we thought we got rid of the evidence. We put it in the garbage.

Control of the victims is an important aspect of the robbery. Weapons are one way of gaining immediate control and one which is likely to reduce resistance (Skogan, 1978). Restraint of the victims by blindfolding, tying and otherwise limiting their mobility is a way in which control can be increased. The chance of the victim attacking or escaping is then minimized. Immobilization of the victims also provides the opportunity for the killers to discuss the alternatives of killing the victims or leaving them alive. The rationalizations for killing can be explored at the time of the robbery and the decision can be made outside of the victims' hearing. When victims are thus killed, although they pose no immediate threat to the killers, they use a secondary defensive justification. In robbery homicide these execution killings are referred to as execution-style homicides.

Robbery Homicide in which the Victim Resists or Attempts to Escape

The victim, a 24-year-old man, and his woman friend were walking down the street. Two men grabbed both of them, knocking the woman down and snatching her purse. The victim broke away from one man and ran toward the other, who shot him in the chest.

Three men went to the victim's apartment to talk about renting. Two of them drew guns and the victim's wife screamed. The victim ran to help her with his own gun and all three shot, but only the victim was hit.

In the above cases, the victim actively resisted. In other cases the victim is shot when reaching for money or putting up his hands.

Frequently, when a robbery has been committed, one of the group members will turn and fire a shot while leaving. Ostensibly, this is to keep the robbery victims from following, but then the end result may be deadly for one of the people robbed.

It is difficult to ascertain in the resistance cases whether there was intent to kill or if the act was defensive. In many cases one victim is selected from the others and shot.

> While a holdup was in progress in a private home, a man came to the door. One of the holdup men pulled the door open all the way and told the man to "freeze." The man ran and was shot in the back of the head.

The shooter went back in the house then and shot two other people. Only one of them died.

> Three couples and two other men were sitting in the den. One couple pulled revolvers and robbed the others. Then the woman went to search the house. The man took a shotgun, pointed it at one of the victims and pulled the trigger, but it didn't fire. He then took his revolver and shot the apartment owner and his cohab in the head. Two people escaped out the window. Two of the others disarmed him but he and his lady ran out the door.

David gives his ideas about the interaction stage.

> How people look and act has a lot to do with whether they got hurt or not, but other things are

*important too. I woke one lady up and she kept
asking me not to hurt her. I don't think she really
thought that I would hurt her because of the way I
acted. When we go into a place we act mean and
the people are afraid. But after a while some of
them, like Donald, keep acting mean, but I act
mean and then friendly. Then when Donald goes,
they kind of lean toward me and tell me where
things are, like drugs or money. When we leave I'm
just glad to get out. I'm always scared going in and I
think the other guys are scared too. Like Donald, he
always hangs back and lets the others go first. He
always gets himself in a position where he can
escape and he won't get hurt. The guys don't say
too much before the crime goes on because you
never know what you're gonna get into.*

In cases where the victim(s) makes an overt action
toward the killers or attempts to leave the scene, we
define the situation as threatening to the killers and to
accomplishing their goal of completing a robbery and
escaping. Under these conditions, the killing may be
justified as a defense action. Killers will often make
statements in their accounts to the effect that the victim
was moving toward them, grabbed their arm or appeared
to be reaching for a weapon. They justify the killing of a
victim who is attempting to escape, in some cases, in a
secondary defensive way. Accounts explain that the victim was seen as going for help or for the police. In cases
in which the threat is not an overt aggressive act toward
the killers, such as opening a closet door or dresser
drawer perhaps to reach a weapon, it is a problem-
solving act. Even in cases where the victim is seen as
going for a weapon, there is time for selection of alterna-

tive actions, as David points out. The killers have the choice of leaving the scene themselves.

THE POST-HOMICIDE PERIOD

In David's group the members talked after the crimes about what happened. Then they relaxed and kidded around with each other. After one robbery homicide, Donald teased Dwayne about beating an old man to death. One of the newer members of David's group, Tony, tells of being with Donald at the time of the killing and what happened afterwards.

Donald told the victim, "Well, we gonna kill you 'cause you won't give us any money." He stopped the car in the middle of the street and turned the radio way up. Then he stuck the .45 to his hip; that's where he shot him. He shot him there once then he kept drivin' around. He drove around 'til he found an abandoned house where nobody stayed. People were stayin' in the house next door. There was a dog in the yard, you know. So we got the guy out and we walked across the street, across a field over to this house. We walked him into this house and Donald laid him on the floor and said, "Go outside and see if you see anybody." As I was going down the steps he didn't give me a chance to see if anybody was alert, if anybody was around. He just shot him in the head. The reason why I know he shot him in the head was he told me so when we got in the car. He said, "Look man, don't tell. Don't say nothin' about it. Don't ever say nothin' about what you doin', O.K.? Word gets around, you're gonna end up in jail for life, for murder." I don't say nothin'. I don't know what to say. This was the

*first time I was with somebody that was killed you
know. Like then he kept talking like he said, "Be
cool, I'm gonna take you home." I said, "Man, like
ain't you givin' me no money, man." He said, "Like
I ain't givin' you no money, man." I said, "Like I'm
always doin' somethin' for you and can't never get
paid and can't never get no money." He said, "Like
man, I'll pay you later. Sooner or later man." I said,
"Like forget about that, you just killed somebody
man." Then he started talkin' valiant. I said, "Man,
you ain't gotta talk valiant to me. Callin' me punk,
sayin' you better not say nothin." It seemed like it
was a threat all along but he say these words to me
before cursing me out. I said, "Why don't you talk
to me like a man." Then he brought it up again two
or three days later. He say, "Man, are you all right
now?" I said, "What do you mean?" He said, "Get
in the car, man." I got in the car and we drove
around and he was steady talkin' to me about the
case as though he was really worried I might tell
somebody what he'd done, about what we done did.
He was just tellin' me to be cool and not say nothin'
to nobody.*

Most of the time, in David's group, they just split the
money and went on home or went wherever they were
staying. The regular group members knew and the new
ones were made to understand that they were not to talk.
In the above case, Tony did not even receive any of the
money taken from the victim.

Robbery homicides occur usually in three short se-
quences. They are briefly planned, executed, and finally,
the loot is divided and the weapons and cars gotten rid of,
after which the group members part until the next time.

SUMMARY

In this section the sequential action of robbery homicide was examined. It was pointed out that in some robberies the decision to kill is clearly made as part of the plan. In other cases, all members are not informed of murder plans, but those who do decide to kill expect the other members to go along with them. Different members have different motives for participating in the group. The attitudes of the group members strongly influence the way they respond to one another in any situation. The fact that the group's norms are criminal makes it easier to become involved in homicide. They start out with an approval of theft and the use of force. They think of the victim as a disrespected and impersonal target. The groups that gravitate to murder appear to have both a leader or strong faction that wants to kill and others who are not strongly resistant. There seems to be a pattern where a group moves into robbery homicides when at least two of the core members become willing to kill. The other members then go along with the killing, but do not develop a killer self-concept and try to avoid participating in the actual killing as much as possible. The other group members seem to maintain their self-identification as robbers while the killers incorporate their role into their identities.

Chapter 5 examines the cases in which the intent to kill is the primary objective.

5 Executions, Contracts, and Revenge Killings

To speak of an execution is, essentially, to speak of pre-meditated killing. An execution, by definition, is the killing of a person who has been judged and sentenced to death. In many execution murders the judge(s) and the executioner(s) are the same person(s). Contract killings are murders in which the judges hire others, often professionals, to do the execution. In Detroit, the issuance of a contract is called "putting out a paper" on a person or persons. The price paid ranges from $200 to $5,000, although occasionally it may range from $50 to $10,000. Professionals usually charge at least $5,000. The price depends, however, on the number of victims, how dangerous the victims are, the likelihood of repercussions from friends or associates of the victims, and a variety of other considerations. The killer is called a "hit" man. Some organizations, such as certain organized crime and drug groups, keep their own killers employed for regular use. Most hit men, however, hire out by the job to any reasonably secure employer.

Execution murders often occur without warning in the street, in the victim's home, or in a car. The street execution contains very little in the way of interaction between the victim and the killers. This is a type often portrayed in gangster movies. Many well known crime figures, such as Albert Anastasia and Joey Gallo, have met their deaths in quick executions. More recently, some of the murders committed by battered wives upon their husbands have taken on the qualities of the execution murder. A battered wife, such as Francine Hughes,[1] judges her husband, finds him guilty, sentences him to death and carries out the execution when the victim is in a defenseless position.

The major differences between the execution murder and legal executions are: (1) the lack of due process; (2) the lack of impartiality of the judging parties; (3) the fact that the judge and executioner are in some cases the same; and (4) the fact that the person being executed is usually unaware of being sentenced or even of having committed a crime.

The major similarity between an execution murder and a legal execution is that there is clearly a judgment of the person and a death sentence passed and carried out.

Robbery homicides in which the victims are bound and gagged are referred to as execution-style. Actually, any pre-meditated murder—any contract murder—any robbery or sex murder in which there is intent to do away with the victims is an execution.

---

1. In 1977, Francine Hughes of Lansing, Michigan, after many years of living with an abusive husband, waited until he fell asleep and poured gasoline on his bed and set fire to it. She was found not guilty by reason of temporary insanity. *Detroit Free Press*, Nov. 4, 1977.

DIFFERENCES BETWEEN ROBBERY HOMICIDES AND EXECUTIONS

Clearly there is an essential difference between the robbery murder and the execution murder in that the primary intent in the execution is the killing of the victim. In many execution-style robberies, it is difficult to determine the primary intent. On occasion, executions are made to look like robberies.

There seems also to be a difference between robbery murderers and contract killers in the degree to which they are ready to kill. Robbery murderers often leave witnesses knowingly because they do not want to kill anymore. Hit men try to avoid situations where witnesses may be able to identify them. Hit men, however, are not as likely to decide to kill on the spur of the moment and will sometimes go to great lengths to avoid killing someone who is not a part of the contract. Some of the important differences between robbery homicides and executions are:

1. In executions, the victim(s) is of primary importance.
2. In robbery homicides, live witnesses are often left unintentionally or because the killing was perceived as defensive. In executions the victim is often selected from a group.
3. In executions the killer(s) always comes armed.
4. Executions usually are more thoroughly planned. Robberies are often planned as they progress.
5. Robbery homicides are likely to have more offenders involved.
6. Hit men tend to consider themselves more elite, superior to robbery murderers, even though they involve themselves in other crimes. The "killer" role identity is central to their self-images.

THE DATA

This chapter examines the second largest type of felony homicide—executions and contract killings. Of the 1974 Detroit cases, 110 were classified as executions. Execution was a common practice in Detroit in the '70s as it was during the gang wars of the '30s. The accounts in the cases are supplemented by some comments by Ricardo who described himself, and was described by the police, as a hit man.

TASKS IN EXECUTIONS AND CONTRACT MURDERS

TASKS IN EXECUTION KILLING

- *deciding to kill*
- *planning*
- *getting equipment*
- *locating the victim(s)*
- *killing, disposing of body*
- *escaping*

TASKS IN CONTRACT KILLING

- *setting up the contract (getting out a paper)*
- *selecting/interviewing personnel*
- *planning*
- *getting equipment; locating additional personnel*
- *locating target, "stalking"*
- *arranging transportation*
- *getting victim into killing location*
- *killing; disposing of the body*
- *getting away*
- *collecting fee*

The tasks in contract killings are more involved because the killer is an employee and has to deal with the employer both before and after the killing. The revenge or gangland slayings that are handled by the injured party or the boss involve the execution tasks. If they are assigned to other persons, however, they involve much the same activities as the formal contract.

The roles in executions and contracts are much more specific. In most cases, the killer or killers are specified. Tasks may be delegated to other persons, as may the actual contracting arrangements. The key role in execution killings, of course, is that of the shooter. It is generally expected that the person accepting the contract will handle the killing.

TYPES OF EXECUTIONS

Below, several kinds of executions will be discussed.

THE QUICK HIT

The first type, the quick hit, is most often used by professionals. The killer wants to do his job as quickly as possible. Occasionally, "hit men" are sadistic and will torture and abuse their victims, but this is rare. Torture killings are usually a result of trying to extract information from victims or to punish them for past actions. Joey states as one of his rules, ". . . you do not torture a man; we're not his judges, just his executioners, and you do not rob him" (Fisher, 1976:63). These are Joey's personal rules and do not hold for others, even in so-called "Mafia" killings. In a number of alleged Mafia killings in recent years in Detroit, the victims have been tortured or mutilated. However, these were cases in which the victim had violated the organization rules and the torture or mutilation was probably meant to serve as an example to others. The other types discussed will be multiple killings, re-

venge/torture executions and contract killings. Following are quick hit situations:

1. There is a knock on the door of the home. The victim
   answers. A voice asks, "Are you Richie Mann?" The
   victim answers "yes" and shots are heard.
2. The victim leaves for or returns from work and is
   found dead next to his or her car in the vicinity of the
   house or place of work.
3. The victim is seated in a bar or restaurant. Sometimes
   the killers order something, but usually they don't
   remain long. They walk over, shoot, and leave.
4. The victim is parked in a car or driving the car. The
   killer runs up to the car and shoots the victim there.
5. The victim is walking along the street, a car slows
   down and one of the passengers shoots.

In most of the above situations, an effort is usually
made by the killer(s) not to hit anyone but the target
victim. That is, they will push bystanders out of the way
or warn them back. For the most part then, if more than
one person is hit, it is probably intentional. In these
cases, there are often people present who see the killers
and witness the killing but are left unharmed. Thus,
even in cases where there might be some benefit to the
killer, the victim is selected from others and there is no
additional, unnecessary, or unintended killing for its
own sake. A witness who identifies the killer and
chooses to testify at that point may be intimidated or
killed. Much of the evidence in these cases comes from
informers or persons who are involved in the case and
who make a deal with the police. This type of killing or
"hit" is done by professionals who are not, in most
cases, known to the victims. The victim is identified or
pointed out and there is little or no interaction between

the victim and killer(s). Occasionally, a short message is delivered. If the victim realizes what is going to happen, often he or she will attempt to dissuade the killer, but there is little time. Many unsolved homicide cases have the appearance of the quick hit.

MULTIPLE HITS

Multiple hits are most common when criminal groups are competing for some type of crime activity or territory. These were frequent during the prohibition period, and during the 1970s in the battle for control of narcotics in Detroit. Multiples are also common in robberies, frequently when the victims know the killers, or when there is resistance.

Multiple hits may occur (a) simultaneously in several locations at once; (b) in relatively rapid succession in different locations; or, (c) with all the victims found or brought to the same place. The logistics of multiple hits are extremely complex if more than two victims are intended. The intent of multiple hits is usually to punish a number of people who have done some kind of "wrong" to the person ordering the hit to get rid of business competition, or to prevent further vengeance from a specific hit.

PUNISHING A GROUP

The following is the description of a group punishment torture execution by a survivor. Ten people were involved in this case. Two were killed, one critically wounded and left for dead, and one wounded slightly. It began in the hotel where the witness, Debra, was visiting with her friend, Carol, and two men, Red and Douglas. She describes what happened.

All of a sudden, about 1 o'clock, someone knocked
on the door. It was Michael and his girlfriend, Mariel. Douglas let them in and they sat on the bed and
talked for about ten minutes. They were all just
talking and then Michael went to the bathroom.
Red was just about to make a phone call. Michael
came out of the bathroom with a gun. I think it was
a .38. He held it in both hands. He said, "Don't
nobody move. Put the phone down and don't say
nothing." Mariel pulled a gun from her coat pocket
and said, "That's right—don't nobody move." She
went to the door and opened it. Michael whistled
and four more people came in. Michael told Douglas, "Nobody crosses me." All of them had pistols
and one had a carbine, one had a shotgun. There
was Juneboy and his wife, Patricia, Walker, Billy
Joy, Henry, and Sharon, Juneboy's sister. They all
started tearing up the room looking for some stuff,
jewelry that Douglas had stolen from them, worth
$9,000. Patricia was cursing at Carol about Carol
wearing some of Patricia's clothes that had been
stolen. Douglas said, "I'll give you the stuff, man.
It's right here in the room." They started hitting all
of them but me. They were hitting them on the head
with guns and kicking them. Then they tied the
three of them with their hands behind them and
gagged them. They took us outside and put us in
separate cars. They put Carol in the trunk of a little
yellow car, and put me in the front seat of the same
car. Patricia and Walker got in the car with me.
Douglas and Red were put in a black Cadillac that
Michael was driving. Then we drove around for a
while. Patricia put a blindfold on me and I asked
her what was she gonna do. I said, "I didn't have

nothing to do with any of this." Patricia said they
weren't gonna do nothing to me. They took us to a
place, an apartment. I still had the blindfold on.
They made the three of them lay on the floor and
sat me on something. I think it was a bed. All six of
them were there talking. I heard Billy J., I think it
was, say, "Come back here, motherfucker, 'fore I
shoot you in the back of the head." Juneboy and
Patricia kept telling Walker, "Shoot them again,"
and somebody said, "Pour acid on them." Then, I
heard Walker say, "Let's go and get out of here."
They left, all but two, I couldn't tell which ones.
One of them said, "What about Debra?" and the
other said, "She wasn't in on it" and I fell on the
floor. Then someone came and said, "Come on
hurry, let's get moving." My hands were tied, but
not too good and I got them loose and took off the
scarf they blindfolded me with. Douglas said, "Help
me up." I said, "I can't help you. I'm gonna call the
police." I looked out to see if the cars were still
there and I didn't see them so I left the building and
ran toward the main street. As I ran, I saw a black
Cadillac turn the corner and stop. I saw the car
door open and started running back to the building.
I saw a man behind me. He started shooting. I
heard four or five shots. One hit my head, one hit
my right arm and hit my left finger. I heard him run
back to the car and I heard the car drive off.

In this case, two people were killed, one remained para-
lyzed, another was wounded, but recovered. None of the
ten people were past their middle 20s; all, with the
exception of two of the women, had extensive records.
All were drug users. No one was convicted because the

witness did not appear. The procedure for gaining entrance was similar to that of robbery homicides. Two people, who were not suspected, gained entrance and surveyed the situation. The tactic of going to the bathroom is used quite frequently, as it allows a group member to draw a pistol and gain control of the situation.

What held them back? It is obvious that, although the group did not want to kill Debra, after they left the apartment they evaluated the situation and decided that she knew too much. So they came back after her. They left her alive, however, and left one of the victims alive in the apartment. This discrimination and hesitation to kill "innocent" people occurs frequently in both amateur and professional cases and is a key factor indicating the rationality, control and decision making in felony homicide cases.

MAINTAINING ILLEGAL BUSINESS CREDIBILITY

The second example is something similar—an unresolved incident involving drugs and money. In both of these cases there is some ego involvement. Not only are the people who are executed judged guilty and sentenced for committing a crime, they have committed a personal affront to the person who engineers the punishment. Since the goods, property and money involved in these cases are usually illegally obtained in the first place, the persons from whom they are taken have no recourse to the law.[2] The following case illustrates the actions that led up to the contract for a multiple victim revenge execution. Some say that Melissa was dating Billy J. and left him for his partner, the Candyman. After

---

2. In a number of cases, however, where someone has been shot during a dope pad ripoff, the pad owner has successfully pleaded self defense. Of course, the person who executes a cheat or thief does not escape prosecution.

that, Billy J. accused Candy of messing up, or ripping off some of his drugs. So Candy went to Billy J.'s store and held a gun on him to straighten him out, but didn't shoot him. Most others say that the trouble started at a party given by Main Man who was the drug supplier for Billy, Candy, and four or five others.

Main Man's story:

> On Saturday I gave a party at my place. There was Billy J. and his women, Marcia and Sandy, a friend of his named Jerome, James Johnson, Roosevelt Taylor, Candyman, Melissa Baker, a girl named Bernadane, my wife, Andrea, Cat Super and his wife, Bobbie. Then later Butch Wilson and Lonnie Burgess came in. Earlier just Roosevelt, Billy J., Candyman and I were at the house. We left and when we got back there was $900 missing from my bedroom. After we discovered the money missing, everyone at the party was searched. I think it was Billy J. that suggested searching everyone. We didn't come up with the money. Finally it was decided the only one that had been upstairs that could have taken the money was Billy J. Candyman called him on it and insisted that he took the money. Candy sent Butch and Lonnie to his pad downtown to pick up his carbine. This was a trick to get Billy J. to come up with the money. It worked too, because Billy finally agreed to give us $1,000 that he had at his boutique. He still kept on insisting he didn't take it. Billy J. left the party and returned and gave over $700 and everyone went home.

Bernadane, who was a witness in the case, gives this account.

That night at Main Man's party I was there when it was discovered that some money was missing. Candyman figured the only one that could have taken it was Billy J. Billy started acting strange and was trembling. Billy started crying and finally said he wanted to show good faith. He said he would get $900 and bring it back. Billy left and returned with some money. He was very upset about being discovered and very disturbed at Candyman for having figured out who took the money. Billy J. was doing a lot of talking about killing Candyman. Candy was upstairs and Billy began pleading with Main Man to give him a gun. He said, "I'll kill him. I'll kill him. I'll give you $1,000 if you let me kill him. Man, let me take that nigger over to the park. I won't kill him here, I'll take him over there." Main Man said, "No," Billy said, "O.K., you watch and see. I'll have something did to that boy or my name ain't Billy J." Last time I saw Candyman he said he went to Billy's shop and confronted him about the threats.

Another witness, Marcia, describes the events as follows:

About a half hour after me, Sandy, and Billy J. arrived at Main Man's party, it was discovered some money was missing from upstairs. It was said to be about $900. Candyman said, "Somebody coming by later to pick up that money and if it's not here, somebody get taken out." Candy was mad and he jumped on his woman and said she was stupid for letting somebody get that money. Candyman told everyone that no one was coming in or getting out until the money was found. He told two men

who were at the party to stand at the front and back
door and not let anyone in or out. The men at the
doors had guns and so did Candyman. Candyman
searched everyone. After Billy J. was searched,
Candyman asked him if he had a gun. Billy went to
Sandy and got his gun from her purse and gave it to
Candyman. Candy said the money that was missing
was for the dope. He asked if the people at the
party had any money they could pitch in and help
pay for it. It was about this time that Candyman
accused Billy J. of taking the money. Billy denied
that he took the money. Billy, Candyman and
Candyman's woman went upstairs and closed the
door. After a short while all three of them came
down. Billy said he was going to the car and get
some money. Sandy, Melissa and I were told by
Candyman that we could not leave. Billy was gone
about 30 minutes and when he got back he counted
out the money and it came to about $900, which he
handed to Main Man. When Candyman came downstairs he placed some drugs on the table in the living
room and Main Man's woman mixed it and the
guests were told to help themselves and have a good
time. Most of those present indulged in the drugs
and Melissa must have had too much because she
passed out and had to be helped when we left. Billy
paced the floor because he was mad and was asking
when he could leave. Finally, around 5 o'clock,
Candyman said it was all right to go. Billy J., Melissa, Sandy and me left together and went to the
shop. Later when Billy, Sandy and I were in the
shop, Billy J. said, "That nigger don't pay me back
that money, I'm getting a paper out on him."

About four days later Billy told me and Jerome

*that he was getting a contract out. Then about a
week before Melissa and Candy were killed Billy
told me to stay in the shop while he and Sandy
went somewhere. They came back in a little while
with two men. All four of them started to leave in
about fifteen minutes to get a blow and I asked
Sandy who the men were. Sandy said, "Those are
the guys Billy lined up to hit Candyman and Melissa. A couple days later Billy J. told me and
Sandy, "I paid those two dudes off and they got
their orders." The next day I saw the men hanging
around the corner from about nine in the morning
until about seven that night. A couple days later I
saw the two of them go in the shop with Melissa
and Candyman about 2 o'clock in the afternoon.
Billy closed the shop after about a half hour and
didn't open again until that night. When I saw
Billy J., I asked him how come he closed the shop
and he said those guys took care of some of the
business with Melissa and Candy right there in the
basement.*

The bodies of Melissa and Candyman were found in a
wooded area about 30 miles from Detroit. They were
gagged and blindfolded. Their bodies had a number of
abrasions, fractures and several burn marks. Both had
been shot in the head.

When they were missing, it was immediately suspected on the street that Billy J. had made good his
threat. Did Billy J. finally get permission from Main
Man? Why was Melissa included in the contract? The
chances are good that Billy did, in fact, clear the contract with Main Man, as there was another rumor on the
street that Candy had quit the dope business. As for

Melissa, was she only included because she had rejected Billy J.?

It is clear in these cases that both personal and business motives are involved. There are several considerations in criminal cases that lead toward justifying homicide. First, criminal business is handled without recourse to courts and written contracts so that in order to conduct business there must be a combination of trust and the threat of force. In a situation where someone takes money from another, or humiliates that person publicly, the person loses face. If they do not take forceful action, they will be perceived as fair game to be ripped off by anyone. Thus, in order to maintain the business, action must be taken. Second, most criminal subcultures generally accept the norms that "anyone who messes with your person, family or money" must be punished (Brown, 1965). Third, there is a loose community of criminals, particularly among the drug subculture, and any type of conflict or confrontation will be "on the street"[3] as soon as it happens. The behavior and outcomes will go far beyond just those present.

In these two multiple gangland executions the personal and profit motives were mixed. Illicit goods were involved in both cases. Thus reporting to the police was not considered as an alternative. The first case was handled personally as a punishment execution by the offended party and his group. The punishment was extended to an entire group rather than only the person most responsible. In the second case, probably because of the complex interrelationships of the drug group, a

---

3. One of the major themes discussed in criminal groups is the fact that business, both personal and criminal, is done "on the street." There is a recognition of the existent criminal community and its information network. There is also an indication of concern for others' opinions. Criminals are aware, too, that a large proportion of cases are resolved through tips to the police.

contract was made with professional killers. Women were involved in both of these cases as both victims and perpetrators and performed the same victim and perpetrator roles as the men.

PROCESSES INVOLVED IN CONTRACT KILLING

In defendants' accounts of killings, they often mention having heard that someone had a contract on them. It appears from their discussions that contract killings are a part of their common understanding. In criminal subcultures, they may be one of the expected results of disagreements over business practices. Most people outside of criminal groups would not know how to go about finding and hiring a killer.

Needless to say, as all activities involving killing are illegal, advertising and contracts are all verbal. Specifically, in order to hire someone to commit a murder, the contractor or killer has to make it known that he is in business; the person or group who want the killing done must let it be known that they are in the market, and the two must get together and make an agreement before the murder can take place. The career contingencies for professional killers are discussed in a later chapter.

PUTTING OUT A PAPER

There are several ways in which contractors and killers may come together. Those organizations that have killers on salary simply call the employee in and give instructions about who the victim is. Those who are hiring freelance killers usually use one of three methods. The first is to announce that they are looking for a killer. Using this method, the victim's name is rarely known, although often it can be guessed. A friend or acquaintance informs them that the killer accepts the contract. The second method is to approach someone directly who is known to be a hit man and ask if he is interested in doing a job. The third method is to approach someone who is known to be a criminal, especially one who is known to have committed some form of violent crime, and ask him if he is interested in a contract.

NEGOTIATING A CONTRACT

Avery, a member of an execution group, discusses the setting of the contract.

> I had heard that four days before the killing Red and Elroy had an argument about some dope Elroy had gotten from Red. They were in Red's after-hours joint. Red got hot about his money and pulled a gun on Elroy. He told him that he would kill him if he didn't have his money tonight. The two of them pushed and shoved each other, then Elroy left. A couple days later Elroy came over to my house. It was about 4:30 or 5:00 in the afternoon. Elroy said to me, "I hear you can do things." I said, "Yeah, what's the deal?" Elroy said, "I'm going to have to kill this nigger." I asked him, "Who's the guy?" and he said, "Red." I said, "Yeah, the guy down the street offered me a thousand dollars to take him out." I agreed to go with him because I was going to collect from the other guy. Jo Jo was at my house at the time but he didn't hear us talking."

In this case, the killer not only had a profit motive, but was able to extend the "doing a public service" rationalization to include helping out a friend. Actually it was a reciprocal arrangement in which the victim had antagonized several parties who wanted him punished. The killer had accepted the contract and had teamed up with the other party, the latter being willing to involve himself directly in the killing. Notice that the depersonalization of the victim is shown by referring to him as "this nigger," rather than by his name.

The next case is described by Henry, a person who was hired in at least six contract killings commissioned by the same person. Henry, too, shows that he has objectified and depersonalized the victims by referring to the "two girls," saying that he has forgotten their names. In this case, the planning was done jointly by Henry and his boss, and they specified how and when the killing would be done.

Henry describes the negotiation stage of one of his contracts.

Edward and Johnny approached me saying they had a person who needed to be killed and did I want the job to do it. The next time Johnny said, "Do you want to make some quick money? Me and Edward have hooked up a deal for killing two girls." I forget their names. I think one of them was Coleen. I'm not sure. Me and Johnny had a somewhat meeting about it and he said how he wanted it done. Like he said he wanted their throats cut so it would look like somebody had robbed the store and took all the money and didn't have any choice but to kill the two girls. I said, "Why not just shoot them?" He said, "No, it wouldn't look right. Plus, it's too close to the place next door and the wall between isn't thick enough to absorb the sound." I didn't ever talk to Edward about this but I understood from Johnny that Edward was going to be the one paying the money, and Edward is the one that paid $8,000 after the job was done.

Ricardo is an experienced hit man for what he labelled "the black mafia." He also runs a flourishing drug business. He described, in an interview, the climate for killing in Detroit and how arrangements were made for his contracts.

A person don't think nothin' about killin' somebody here in this city. It's about the law and slick talkin' lawyers and money. If a person has money he can get off any kind of offense. See, as it is right now, a person will come out better having a murder case than having an armed robbery case or a rape case because murder is so hard to prove, you see, and the majority of people that commit murders, if they have a witness they eliminate the witness. They buy him off. Have him taken out. You can have a person taken out here for $300 — it's just that easy 'cause there's so many people here that for $1,000 they'll kill two or three people. I'd usually take care of my business and go out. I'd come back home. I might have a call from these people saying like, 'get in touch with me—very urgent' or something. So, I'd go out to his house. He might have a ticket or something for me and my partner to fly to California and he might tell us that so and so is goin' out there to pick up a half a key of dope and the people out there gonna call us and let us know when he be in, so we can go out there and take care of him out there and come on back and that's it. In the course of a week, every two weeks, we had two or three people. Like if they would say O.K. $10,000 for John Doe. Like

*most of the time they'd give the people half the
money and like after you'd bring back some of the
jewelry or something of a certain individual or
something to let them know you took care of this
business, like then you get the other half but me,
like I was getting mine right up front.*

In all the above negotiations, the person who wanted
the job done contacted the killer and offered the job at a
particular price. In some cases there is discussion of
location and methods. Usually the killer can refuse if the
money isn't right or if he has some reluctance to commit
any murder or one particular murder. There may be
some pressure on the employee, or he may be persuaded
in some cases. Once the agreement is made, however,
the contract must be kept.

THE HOMICIDE INTERACTION

In most cases, the contractor and the killers are not in
touch until the job is done. The case of Elroy is the
exception. The following cases illustrate the homicide
interaction in contract killings.

Avery describes the group interaction in the killing of
Red.

*After I had agreed to go with Elroy, we got into his
brother's car. There was me, Elroy, his girlfriend
and his brother, Dan. We rode around the down-
town area and to all of Red's joints looking for him.
We rode around for six or seven hours and we
couldn't find him. So we called it off for the night.
The three of them dropped me off at my house. The
next day at about 6:30 in the evening, Elroy and his
brothers, Dan and Adam, came over to my house.
The four of us discussed killing Red and how we*

we would kill him. We left my house. Elroy was driving. We went over to Adam's house and drank a little wine; then we left. When we left, me and Adam got into a Pontiac. Adam was driving. Elroy and Dan got into a Chrysler that belonged to Adam. We followed them down the street to where we saw Red in front of his place. Elroy slammed on his brakes and Adam drove down the street past where Red was standing and stopped in the alley. Adam got a shotgun that was in the back seat. I was watching Elroy and Dan. They had stopped the car in front of the place. Dan jumped out of the left door with a sawed-off shotgun and fired both barrels. Elroy got out. He had a .22 rifle and a .38 revolver. He fired some shots on the outside of the store then he went into Red's place. Red had spun around and fallen through his front door when the shotgun blast went off. I heard some more shooting in the place. After the shooting had stopped we looked up and saw two policemen in the alley behind a garbage can shooting at us. Adam told me to get from behind the wheel and let him drive. I got from behind the wheel and Adam jumped over the seat and got behind the wheel. I saw Elroy and Dan come out of Red's store and they ran the other way. We drove that way and were waiting for them. One of them threw a gun out the window. We stopped on Woodward and split up.

In the above case, the group planned on a quick hit. They intended to seek out the victim in, or near, one of his known hangouts or places of business. They discussed how they were going to do the hit in the car, as they looked for him. When they did not accomplish the killing on the first attempt, they met the next day and planned it in a little more detail. They did not, however, fire on the police who were shooting at them. It is part of the general mythology among criminals, with some basis in fact, that the police are not too concerned when they kill each other, as long as no innocent bystanders are involved. But if a police officer is killed or injured, the police won't rest until those responsible are put away. So, in spite of the fact that they were armed, and outnumbered the police, they fled.

INTERACTION BETWEEN THE VICTIM AND THE KILLERS

Ricky describes the homicide interaction between group members and the victim in another contract hit.

> Wesley had told me he had a contract on Reginald and did I want to go with him. I said, "yes." I knew Reginald from prison. Wesley said to be at his house at 10 o'clock. I went to his house at 8 o'clock and we sat around until 10. There was me, Wesley, James, and Jessie. We sat around and talked and drank. We went to the hotel in two cars and went to Stephen's room. There was a girl, Jeanie, there. Wesley got a gun and cleaned it off and loaded it and we came down to another room. Gregory was there. Wesley asked Gregory if he could get the guy over and Gregory said "yes." Gregory called a guy named Willie and told Willie he had a fresh shipment in that day and he wanted Willie to try some but he didn't want him to bring the other two guys that he brought earlier that day. While we were waiting Wesley arranged things to his liking. He told me to sit there. He told James to stand by the

door and he had Gregory over to the side with some drugs on an album. He said that when they came in, after they sat down, when he got up and went to the toilet and came back and sat down, that was the arrangement to seize them. About ten minutes later there was a knock on the door and Reginald and Willie came in. Willie sat to my left and Reginald to my right. We started talking and Gregory gave Willie some drugs. Wesley got up and went to the toilet and when he came back I got up and forced Reginald to the floor. I seen he had a gun in his pocket and I taken that. Wesley seized Will and put him on the floor. We was standing up over him and Wesley took the pistol and started beating Willie on the head. In the process of Wesley hitting Willie about the head with the pistol, the gun discharges and went through my leg and hit Gregory. I said, "Won't the police come, man?" Wesley said, "Naw, they won't come because like this hotel is owned by _____ ." Then we took Reginald downstairs and put him in a car, me and James and Wesley. We taken him over to Thomas's house. Reginald was on the floor in the back and I was in the back with a pistol in his mouth. Wesley had a pistol pointed at Willie. Thomas put alcohol on my leg and we left. On the way out the door I asked Thomas what we gonna do with Reginald and he looked and said, "Take him out." It was up to him because it was his contract. Wesley directed James to back up into an alley and he told Reginald that he was letting him go and for him to get out of the car and for him to keep his hands on his head. Then he shot him in the head twice. I asked Wesley did he need any help with Willie and he said, "No."

*the head twice. I asked Wesley did he need any
help with Willie and he said, "No."*

In this case, the hit man selected his personnel, arranged transportation and a safe location, then arranged to have the victim brought to him. Before the victim was brought in, he positioned his team in various locations in the room and arranged signals for attacking the victim. In spite of the careful arrangements, he accidentally discharged his gun as he was administering a beating to the victim. They then took the victim to the contractor to get a final "O.K." on the execution.

As we examine execution cases, it appears that the lengthier the interaction and the more complicated the instructions to the hit team, such as administering punishment or transporting the victim to different locations, the more likely it is that there will be a foul-up in the plan. Executions that involve torture, punishment, or the securing of information from the victims, generally require a larger killer group and tend to have less predictability than the quick hits. Professional killers like to control the situation in every way possible and prefer contracts in which they decide on the arrangements. Most seem to agree, however, that the details are the prerogative of the person(s) paying for the contract. These persons may specify weapons, locations and time schedules.

CONTROLLING THE VICTIMS

The next case is another contract carried out by Henry and his son. This is the case discussed earlier by Anthony (pp.24-26). Anthony was first invited to take part in the executions. As he refused, Henry took one of his son's friends with him. One of the victims escaped and

Anthony accompanied Henry in an attempt to finish the job.

Henry tells how he interacted with the victims in a case where two were killed and one intended victim escaped.

The guys I took with me were my son, Henry Junior, and a friend of his named George. I don't know his last name. When the two girls were there we were gonna stick them and put water in the tub and hold them under 'til they stopped breathing, then when Lonnie got there with the money we'd grab him. Like we'd have had time to have found the money and the dope by then. We take the money from Lonnie and drown him in the bathtub too and turn the gas on in the apartment and leave.

We had to knock on the door—there's an inside chain lock and Wilma had it on the door. I opened the door— I couldn't push it no farther 'count of the chain and Wilma asked who was it. I said "Henry" and she says, "What do you want?" and I says, "I gotta lay here tonight 'cause Edward comin' by in the morning with some money an' I be leavin' town and he said this would be the coolest place to lay." An' she took the chain off and we came in and she went back to the bedroom where they had the television on and I took the phone an' I made a couple phone calls and I tole her like I was gonna call the store and see if Ed was there and she said, "O.K. but I want to use the phone too." This is when I discovered there's two girls already in the apartment, Wilma and this other girl. I was supposed to kill Wilma and wait for Corry and kill her but this other girl was there. I didn't know her name—it was in the paper and I don't know what it is now. Wilma was supposed to be alone but she had this other girl there and it kinda put a crimp in the plan because Wilma was gonna have to be eliminated before Corry got home. Bein' two girls there already we got kinda confused, you know. Oh, and then there was the baby, there was a baby there. I think it was Wilma's little girl. She was in bed sleeping. Like I made the calls and Wilma came and got the phone and took it back to the room and I followed her and that's when I saw the second girl and the baby. I was standing in the doorway and she introduced me to the other girl, and I said, "Hey, how are ya"—just general conversation. I brought the phone back out and made Wilma come out and get it and it seemed as soon as she did it was Corry wantin' to know did she want something from the store and I instructed Wilma she wasn't to tell Corry I was there and if she did, I would do something bad to her then. I led Wilma to believe it was Corry actually that we came for. Wilma suspected at the time that we all came for her. She didn't say it in words but her expression and the way she acted conveyed the impression that she thought we would hurt somebody. I told her we wanted Corry and that if we got her the other girls wouldn't be bothered and she said, like, "please don't hurt my baby." I said, "I won't, the baby is excluded and you are excluded as long as you do what I tell you to do." She talked to Corry on the phone and told her to bring some milk or some milk and bread, or something. Anyhow, she hung up and we tied the two girls up and sat them on the floor and we looked for Corry. They didn't give us any trouble whatsoever. Like, after I told Wilma what was happening or what was supposed to be happening, she felt kind of reassured, you know. We tied them up with stockings and I think I had some string or rope in my pocket. One had a towel or face cloth on her mouth and I think Wilma had a stocking balled up in her mouth. I don't remember, like it was going real fast and it was almost two o'clock and Corry was going to be getting off from the store and we knew when Corry was going to be getting off from the store and we knew when Corry leaves the store it takes her seven minutes to get from the store to the house. Wilma and the other girl, she started to cry. I took the thing off her mouth and I talked to her and I told her everything will be all right. "Don't worry about nothing" and I put the thing back in her mouth and my son said, "Here comes Corry."

She rung the bell and I pushed the button to let her in and I just told her, like, "Hey, come on. Do just what I tell you and there won't be any trouble." I led her to believe we were waiting on Lonnie. Each one thought I was waiting for the next one and they felt reassured, you know. And I tied Corry up and set her in the bedroom. All three of the girls were setting in the bedroom on the floor and we were waiting for Lonnie. Lonnie was on the list also. If it was possible to kill Lonnie while getting the two girls, it was wanted done. Edward wanted it done 'cause it would strengthen his relationship with his girlfriend, plus it would put a fear in her heart. Actually, the reason he wanted Lonnie killed as well, he never did divulge it but he said enough to let me know he did want Lonnie killed also. I have better control over the three. When Lonnie came in it surprised him. He fell right on the floor. I tied him. I stood him up against the wall and tied him up and went to put a gag in his mouth but one of the girls said or done something in the bedroom that diverted my attention. I looked around again and Lonnie was going out the window. I pulled my gun and went to the window. He might have been almost to the ground. I fired at him. I don't know if I hit him or not but I fired one shot at him and I came back in the room and there I shot the three girls. The gun woke the baby because she started crying. I shot two girls and I think George shot the other one 'cause Junior didn't have no gun. There wasn't but one gun. The other gun we took off Lonnie. When he went to go out the window, it was something like plexiglass, he bounced back, then he hit it again. At that time he went out. I may have shot twice but I don't remember. One of the girls may have been shot twice. I had them bullets with the buckshots or beebees in them and it jammed my gun. This is why I think one of them may have been shot twice because I twirled the cylinder and pulled the trigger. After we shot them, we ran out. I thought Lonnie might be in the area. Just layin' there waitin' for the police so he could make himself known. We circled the block twice. The third time we seen the police car on the corner by the apartment building. We couldn't find the narcotics, they was supposed to be on the shelf in the closet, and we found some one dollar bills under the mattress where the baby was layin'. The money Lonnie had—my son stuck his hand in Lonnie's pocket but I told him to wait, we'd get that later. And we had a

TV and component set out, we was gonna take with us. I called Edward to tell him the job was done. I told him about the extra girl being there. He said, "Don't worry about it. It would just seem like a robbery." We were gonna pay George $2,000 and I told my son I was going to pay him some money and buy his baby some things but between my son and me we didn't decide on an amount.

Henry's account of this case illustrates his actions in calming the victims until he is ready to kill them. As the arrangements made in this case included the time, the location and the weapon, Henry had to wait for the victims to arrive. He did not want to shoot and have the police come. Nor did he want the victims to make noise that might cause the neighbors to investigate. He was able to secure their cooperation by convincing them that they would survive by following his instructions. Henry also provides some of his own speculations on the mixed motives of the person who issued the contract.

Although the murders were planned primarily to collect insurance money, Henry speculates that the contractor may gain some personal benefits from the killings as well. On Henry's part, however, the profit is the entire motive. As Henry describes the homicide, he shows himself as concerned with the emotional state of the intended victims in so far as it will affect the outcome of the interaction. Although Henry thought that he had taken all of the possible problems into account, he was still unprepared for the escape of the third victim. Here, again, the importance of the victim action and the difficulty in predicting what will occur in the actual situation for the killers is emphasized. Once the shooting started, the executions had to be completed quickly so culty in predicting what will occur in the actual situation for the killers is emphasized. Once the shooting started, the executions had to be completed quickly so that the killers could escape before the police arrived. In executions, most killers prefer to use guns as weapons. Guns are dependable and allow the killers to maintain greater distance from the victims. Some hit men try to get their victims to isolated locations so the sound of their shots will not bring the police. Both robbery and execution killers try not to shoot until they are ready to leave the scene of the crime.

CONDUCTING AN INVESTIGATION AND DECIDING THE GUILT OR INNOCENCE OF GROUP MEMBERS

The next case shows that prolonged interaction can cause emotional pressure on members of both the killer group and the victims. The previous cases are accounts of the homicide interaction in contract executions by the killers. The following is an account of the interaction by a female witness after the killers have come in.

Porky and Blood—they put their guns out in front of them and said, "Everybody who is armed, lay their stuff out." I looked at Armando, motioning him not to touch the carbine, you know, and I was leaning, like, I had my pistol under me, like, I had it up under the pillow and Top Dog had his on him. When they come there, all they kept telling Top Dog, "Whatever you do, don't do anything to Blood and Porky." Top Dog said, "Man, what would I want to do anything to Blood and Porky for?" I thought it was you and Maureen coming to talk, you know, all about the diamonds and so they come on. They was no more than fifteen minutes.

There was Blood, Jimmie, Porky, Calvin, Violet, Ernest, and Archie, that was it. I knew all of them except Ernest, or at least I'd seen them 'cause they hang out. No one even mentioned any diamonds yet. I guess Blood and Porky just came to check on Top Dog's mood and when they see it's O.K., to tell the other ones to come out. We're all just sittin' on the bed and when Maureen comes in, she comes around the other side of the bed and sits down and her knee bumps the carbine and she throws the cover off of it. Blood say, "I thought I told you to place all the weapons in the middle of the bed." "No," Armando says, "You said to place the weapons we had on us. I didn't have any on me." We just sitting there talking an' I'm saying what Maureen told me and she's saying what I told her. You know, about in Miami running off with her man. You know, the diamonds still haven't come up. So they were asking about the diamonds and Blood says, "Well, listen, everyone here is guilty until proven innocent." Then they called another guy. He come. They called him D. J. but he had seen Top Dog and Porky over at Porky's house takin' care of business so he thought Top Dog and Porky were good friends an' he said he was trying to get a hold of Top Dog to tell him someone had broken into Maureen's house. He knew the house had been messed up because the screen was missing. Pretty soon then the phone calls started comin' in 'cause they asked how did anyone know that Maureen was leaving town. So I says he told Diane. So he has me pick up the other phone and call Diane. So Diane had talked to me and I had talked to her and she was going all the way and I said, "No. Tell me *exactly what you told me before, exactly what you told me.*" So she talks to her mother-in-law—well, Maureen had called her 'cause they wanted to know how they knew that Maureen was in Miami. So this all comes through over the phone. Then I'm sitting there and another call comes through and it's Richard (my brother-in-law) saying, could he speak to Top Dog. I says, "You can't speak to Top Dog—he takin' care of some very important business." Then Maureen gets on the phone and talks to Diane, and Diane tells her the same thing she had said to me, you know, and Blood heard the same conversation over again. At this time Calvin, Top Dog, Archie, and Porky go out of the room and go straight to the front. Blood doesn't allow me to get up. Archie said, "Be seated. Be seated. Don't move." So I said, "Where's Top Dog?" He said, "They went to Shorty's place to see Richard, or something." During this time they kept me in the back but I could see that Top Dog was gone because the doorbell rang and I went to the door each time it rang. They let Violet and Calvin go. Who was there, was Maureen and D. J. and Archie and Armando and me. I got some clothes out and Blood told me there's no use getting those clothes together and putting them on 'cause you're not going anywhere. I said, "I've got to go to the clinic." He said, "Just put the clothes down and stay as you are." So I just took tranquilizers and fell asleep until Porky shook me awake and asked about some Omar. I says, "I don't know no Omar." Porky and Jimmie had come back with Top Dog. He says, "That's your brother-in-law." I said, "I got a brother-in-law but his name isn't Omar." Jimmie says, "Call your sis-

anything was implicated about the diamonds. So
Jimmie and Porky go in the room and they're
talkin'. So then the phone rang and I have it only I
just break down and start crying. By now it's after 9
o'clock (13 hours). They told me to get dressed so I
got dressed in front of everyone there. I am nervous
and don't know where Top Dog is. Jimmie tells me
he got away from them at Federal Collateral saying
he's got to see his parole officer. They had took him
to all kinds of pawn shops. Now Porky and Jimmie
are sitting in the next room. So I'm nervous and
crying and when the phone rings I can't talk and
Blood tells them to hang up. Nobody needs to know
what's going on. Then Jimmie just snaps. Blood
goes back to see what's going on and Jimmie barri-
cades himself in the john and pulled his pistol on
Blood. It's a P38. I thought it was Top Dog's. I really
didn't know, I wasn't close enough to see, but earlier Jimmie had a smaller gun. He just got on Blood
and told him, "Don't move." He had this other guy
take his pistol off him, then he turned around and
made Porky give up his pistol and Archie give up
his pistol and made them get on their knees. I was
on the phone and just in hysterics. I don't even
know who I'm talking to. I was crying as I was
getting ready to talk. I just say, "If you could see
what I'm looking at" and he says to hang up the
phone. So Jimmie had asked for every gun in there.
So I takes the carbine—it's laying on this side because this is where Blood had been setting. So I go
to pick it up and give it to him so he tell me, "No,
put it down. Don't move. Drop it right there." So I
dropped it, so Armando sitting on the other side, so
he say, "Get out of the way. You're right in the

tell me, "No, put it down. Don't move. Drop it right
there." So I dropped it, so Armando sitting on the
other side, so he say, "Get out of the way. You're
right in the gunfire range." So he got all their pistols. So he makes me come out. Armando in front of
me, Armando got the keys so that makes him have
to open the doors. I'm in back. Armando and Maureen, and Jimmie is in back of Maureen and he's
checking all the rooms. He's got a .45 and a P38.
All I was thinking about was him killing us. He's
got all of us in front of him including Porky. Jimmie's crazy. Porky gets in front of Blood. He says,
"Man, no more, whatever it is don't do it." The
phone rang and Blood picks it up and I heard him
say he's about ready. Blood says, "I'm gonna blow
his brains out—I'm gonna blow the motherfucker's
brains out." So he's talking like this. He told Porky,
"Take his gun off him." Porky, or one of them, they
get in cars and he says everybody goes on Chicago.
Finally it dawns on me. Porky is in front and Blood
in back and we don't see Jimmie, and Blood say, "I
haven't even got my little fuckin' pistol and that
nigger done snapped his mind." He say, "I'm never
goin' over there without a pistol 'cause he'll never
shoot me." Then they started talking and Archie got
out and made a phone call and Blood tells me,
"You know, you're not even implicated anymore."
He said he'd give me $50 to get a cab and go home,
but still I'm ridin' with them. I don't know, like, I'm
still full of those tranquilizers. They pick up some
more pistols and he's telling me "we've got to hold
a meeting on that guy. He knows where the stash is.
He knows where everything is. So we got to hold a
meeting and see what we're gonna do about him

you know." So, now I'm in the car with Archie and Porky and Archie gets out and leaves. He says, "I gotta go. My wife's just had major surgery and I can't be stayin' out like this. I hate to run off like this but I gotta go home." So I stop and get something to drink and we go to the motel (me and Porky) and are drinkin' and I'm tellin' him I gotta go home 'cause I know Jimmie didn't lock my door, an all the time Porky is hitting on me sayin' you know what makes me so mad is you don't remember me. You don't remember me. He says, "You know they'll call me a dirty motherfucker if I mess up Top Dog's women while he's in the penitentiary." I said, "No, they won't say that 'cause you ain't gonna have me."

In the execution of Top Dog, four people were released without being injured. The interaction was prolonged. The account shows that the killers made an effort to conduct an investigation, and only to punish the person who was judged to be guilty. We see the community characteristics of the illicit drug business in Detroit by viewing the depths of their relationships, and the interaction between the different group members. Vern E. Smith, who wrote an award-winning article for *Newsweek* on "Detroit's Heroin Subculture," followed by a fictionalized account of that subculture in *The Jones Men*, emphasized this interactional network. Ricardo also pointed out that the top "dope men" not only did business together, but partied together as well. Although many of the execution killings employ hit men who are unknown to the victim, criminals seek their own revenge or punishment on rip-offs done by acquaintances. These cases tend to have a mixed motive. The insulted party has been deprived of some goods or money and is angry at the thought that someone considers them a mark.

The business transactions may occur among a variety of criminal groups in Detroit. The social interactions tend to be racially, and in some cases, ethnically stratified. These informal networks, which are known both to the criminals and to the police, complicate the homicide interactions. The criminals decide to kill or not to kill associates on the basis of the expected response of the community. In some cases, killing a person who has transgressed against another group will be approved as long as all people killed were directly involved. In the case of Top Dog, the group decided his execution was necessary and justified, and no retribution was expected from his associates.

In all of the above interactions, the victim has some time in which he realizes, or strongly suspects, that he is going to be killed. In some cases, however, it is only seconds. In many of these cases the victim must decide whether to resist or cooperate, whether to act immediately or wait.

THE POST-HOMICIDE PERIOD

After the homicide has occurred, the members of the group usually split up. When group members are relatives or close friends, this may not be the case. Usually the group member who made the contract will inform the person who hired him that the job is complete. In some cases, especially in the drug community, and if the killer is not a regular employee, the killer will have to provide proof of having committed the murder. The method of payment and the necessity for proof varies, as Ricardo said. Ricardo was paid at least part of the money in advance. Ricardo, Joey and other professionals do not usually have problems with payments. They also have arrangements for assistance with bail, etc.

Avery received $300, although he had initially expected $1,000. He still would have to pay his assistants; however, in this case he was not the shooter. Ricky received $100 and $25 for gas. He was supposed to receive additional money later but was arrested before he collected. Henry received $8,000 for one job and was promised another $5,000 that he never collected. Both of the cases discussed were insurance cases. Henry took them expecting that he would be paid when the insurance was collected. He actually collected only $200 beforehand.

In most cases where the killers consider themselves professional, they do not implicate the person who hires them. They expect, and usually receive, help from that person or the organization for whom they work.

SUMMARY

What we learn from this chapter is that certain felony homicides involve doing away with people who have violated some rule, or who are in the way. Execution may be handled by the offended group itself but often is done by hired killers. The killings often are witnessed. But they rarely result in convictions for felony homicide or first-degree murder. In many cases the victims and killers are acquainted. They have a liking, or at least no animosity, toward each other. This makes no difference.

In the next chapter sex homicides and sexual behavior in homicide cases will be examined. An effort will be made to draw some conclusions about sexual homicides.

6 Sex-Related Homicides and Sexual Behavior in Other Felony Homicides

Another important kind of felony homicide occurs in connection with a sexual assault. Although there is no killing for monetary profit as in robbery and contract killings, a similar type of impersonal, predatory and self-seeking behavior is involved. The victim in most sex killings, as is so often the case in robbery killings, is just someone who is in the wrong place at the wrong time. Later in the chapter, sexual assault in other felony homicides will be examined. We shall see how sexual assault is used as another way to humiliate, degrade, and punish victims. The offenders take what they want, without regard for the victims.

The sex homicide, like the other homicides, may be committed by a group or by an individual; however, the offender is more likely to be a lone individual than in other felony homicides. As with robberies, there is some speculation in the sexual assault homicide that the original intent is not to kill. On the other hand, again like robbery homicides, the victim is often killed without anger or as a non-defensive act. It is difficult to see how or if homicide is related to sexual behavior at all. Psychiatrists, beginning with Freud, have long juxtaposed eros and thanatos, or sex and death. No one, however, has been able to demonstrate that there is any direct relationship. Except for a few specific cases, no one has been able to show that the act of killing is sexually arousing. Yet sexual acting out and actual sexual assault often occur in murder cases. In 22 of the 1974 homicides, sex was involved. In 13 of these, it appeared that sex was a motive.

In sex murders, weapons other than guns are used much more frequently than in other felony homicides. We can only guess that this means that murders in sex crimes are even less intentional than murders in robberies. Or it may simply be that the victims are more often lone women and children who are easier prey.

Most sexual assaults do not end in murder. With the exception of those cases where there is obvious pathology,[1] the sex murder usually is in many ways similar to the robbery murder. That is, the victim is killed to allow the killer to escape punishment.

SEX MURDERS

In the following cases the apparent motive is sexual satisfaction. In Detroit, homicide cases with a primary motive of sex usually occur only ten to twenty times per year.

A young, attractive high school teacher met her killer in a neighborhood singles bar. She invited him home with her. The next day friends found her with her throat slashed and a butcher knife inserted with the handle in her rectum. The autopsy report showed that intercourse had taken place.

---

1. Such are the cases where the killer can achieve sexual satisfaction only with dead victims. Actually, psychosis is infrequent in homicides. Levi (1975:4) quotes a figure of 4 percent psychosis rate for U.S. homicides in 1973.

A 65-year-old woman left a restaurant bar at 11 o'clock one evening. Friends waited for her to come back to spend the night with them. The next day she was found in her garage, raped and strangled.

A 20-year-old prostitute went to a motel with a client. The desk man heard hollering and knocked at the door and the noise stopped. She was found the next morning, face down on her knees, with her head resting on her arms, strangled.

Another 20-year-old prostitute was found in a motel with many stab wounds in her chest and with her anus ripped. The desk man heard screams and called the police, but the killer escaped out the window.

In all of the above cases, the victims probably refused to cooperate with the perpetrator in some way and were killed. The general pattern of the killer is sexual molestation. Indifference to the victim here is basically no different from stealing from or killing a victim in business competition. Much of the research on sex offenders indicates that they fall into the following general categories: (1) those who have some inadequacy in the masculine role and are often inept in their sociosexual skills; (2) those who are hostile toward women; and (3) those who include rape or sexual assault among other predatory criminal acts (West, Roy, Nichols, 1978). The feeling of power and control over the victim that the victim's fear creates seems to be a common element in all felony homicides. Most criminals involved in homicides recognize their use of force as a way of both controlling and punishing people. Both the frustrative and malefic definitions of the situation are common in these cases, as the victim is seen as thwarting and often deriding the perpetrator. Depersonalization of the victim is very clear, as the victims are frequently referred to as "cunts," "bitches," etc.

In another case, the killer was living in the home of his girlfriend, Sally.

Sally went out and the rest of the family went to sleep, and he asked the father for his car keys so he could go and look for her. Sally's father said, "No," so he went and got a hammer. He went into the father's bedroom and hit him once with the hammer. Senior raised his arms and said, "Why Leonard?" "I hit him three more times. I went to the kitchen and got the butcher knife and went into Sally's sister Teddie's room. I told her to take off her pants. She ran and woke up her younger brother, Junior. He tried to grab me and I stabbed him. Then I took Teddie back to the bedroom and screwed her. After I screwed her I stabbed her, then I stabbed the baby and senior."

Again, in this case, it appears that the killer simply killed these people because they thwarted him. At no time does he mention being angry, or even thinking of the victims at all.

In another case the killer raped and strangled a six-year-old girl. He says:

Jenny had a piece of glass in her foot. We went into my apartment to get it out. She asked to use the bathroom and come out with her pants down. I started playing around with her and she got excited and stuff. I just eased her pants off and started doing it and she started to scream so I tried to hold her. I put my hands on her mouth and neck because she started to scream when I put my penis in her. She didn't fight me before I started to screw her. She started screaming she hurts. I was afraid the people next door might hear her. I tried to quiet her down with my hands on her mouth. I didn't know she was dead. I thought she had shut up. She didn't move. I went in and used the bathroom and came back. She didn't move or anything and I realized she was dead. I picked her up and put her in the cupboard and covered her with papers and I took off.

In a similar case a teenage boy was left to babysit with his three-year-old niece. He attempted to rape her. When he couldn't, he committed sodomy. When the baby started to whimper, he strangled her.

In these cases the situation becomes important. The killer usually has considered raping the victim, and does it when the opportunity presents itself. In his rehearsal of the crime, he has not usually considered the victim's screaming or resistance or what will happen after. The killing rationalizations in these cases seem to be most commonly future defensive. The murder is a solution to avoid getting caught for the sex crimes.

TASKS IN SEX HOMICIDES

- *selecting the victim*
- *isolating the victim*
- *securing cooperation or immobilizing the victim*
- *performing the sexual act*
- *killing*
- *getting rid of the body or escaping*

The tasks in sex homicides are much more limited than those in either robbery or execution killings. In cases where there is a division of labor, if there are two or more perpetrators involved, it is usually more a matter of taking turns than having separate tasks. One person may hold the victim while the other sexually molests him or her, but there are not necessarily individuated role identities.

SEXUAL ASSAULT IN OTHER FELONY HOMICIDES

The cases discussed thus far have been clearly sex-related. There have been no group members present to respond to the behavior. Two other types of murder in which sex may be involved are the revenge execution and the robbery homicide. First, let us look at a revenge execution.

The participants were two sisters and a male friend. Another couple was also involved. The assault took place at their house. Connie said:

> Lester came to my house and me and my sister, Peaches, went in his car with him. We went to Lester's apartment and he shot some dope and Peaches took a pill, I think. When Lester had picked us up he asked me if I had a gun. I said, "Yes" and went and got it. It is a .45 revolver. I had talked to Lester before and it was understood that we were going to make some money but I didn't know how or what my role would be. The three of us went to Barry and Susan's. Barry and Susan were talking about being robbed and they said that Janice must have done it. Barry, Susan and Lester were saying that they would set the score straight with Janice. Peaches also said that Janice has caused some trouble between her and her boyfriend. They went to a restaurant and found Janice and brought her

back to Barry and Susan's. The four of them began to hit Janice and we took her into the bedroom. Janice was made to take off her clothes and she was made to go down on Peaches while Lester was having sex in her rear. Janice was screaming, "Please don't do this to me. Why you doing this to me? I don't even know you that good. Lester, why you doing this?" Lester said, "Because I like ass. Come on, Janice, show me how you suck a dick." Susan took a baseball bat and put it up inside Janice between her legs while she was hollering. I was holding my gun on Janice and put the gun to her head and told her to be quiet. Barry hit Janice with his fist and so did Lester. Susan hit her on the legs with the bat. Lester and Barry left the room and Susan and Peaches and I continued to hit on her. Someone bumped me and my gun went off. The bullet missed Janice. They were afraid that someone might have heard the shot so they had Janice get dressed. Janice, Peaches, Lester, Barry and I left in Lester's car. Lester kept asking Barry what to do with Janice but Barry kept falling asleep. We stopped on the street and Lester said, "Let her out." Janice and I got out along with Peaches and Lester. Once outside the guns got switched and at one point I had both guns. Lester said to me, "What are you going to do?" I said that I had nothing against the girl but he said, "You do your thing," and he got back in the car. I walked back. Peaches asked me if I wanted to do it and I said, "No, this is between you people, not me." Peaches told Janice to lay down and Janice laid face down. Peaches shot her four or five times. We got back in the car. Lester told me before, "Go and shoot her in the

*head. You have to kill her." He had tried to wake
Barry up to kill her but Barry wouldn't wake up.*

In another case, the victim's wife heard a noise on the
porch.

*She opened the door and a man her husband knew
put a sawed-off rifle to her head. Her husband was
sleeping on the couch. The man told her, "Don't
scream, don't say nothing." He ordered her to the
kitchen and told her to get a butcher knife. Then he
took her upstairs. He told her to cut the phone cord
and tied her with it. He went downstairs and shot
her husband twice in the head as he lay on the
couch. He untied her and brought her downstairs.
She saw her husband on the couch. He was bleeding and it looked to her like his brains were on the
floor. He made her stand in front of her husband
and look at him and told her that the same thing
would happen to her if she didn't do what he said.
He took her back upstairs after getting her husband's car keys from her and his coat and hat. He
raped her and made her commit fellatio on him,
telling her, "Suck it. Remember what I told you."
He retied her hands with the phone cord and left,
taking $200, her husband's coat, hat and car.*

The wife in the case above had been separated from
her husband, who was involved in narcotics. She be-
lieved that his killing was a contract killing. The police
heard rumors, however, that the victim and his killer
had been homosexual lovers. The killer was not convicted in this case. He was later convicted of a double
execution of two other narcotics dealers.

In these cases there is some animosity toward the victim and the sexual acts are used as punishment or torture. In some of the robbery cases, however, the sexual assault seems to occur simply because the victim is there. The offenders may have decided ahead of time that if a woman is there, "I will rape her." In David's group, for example, the rape was an expected part of the robbery. While the homicides for this group occurred in only a few of the robberies, most often when the victim was a drug dealer or resisted, the rape was almost inevitable.

David says that he had several girlfriends, one of whom he lived with part of the time. He reported that Donald also had a girlfriend, but not any of the others. One of the members of the group he particularly disliked he described as "crazy." He illustrates by stating that Mitch once tried to climb up the outside of his house and get into bed with his six-year-old sister. While David considers this "crazy" behavior, he does not consider the rape of victims "crazy." When he talked about rape he said, "I raped her" in the same manner as he said "I drank a coke." He said he felt the same about all manner of crime; it didn't make much difference. Perhaps he thought about the murders a little more because they were all aware that "you could get a lot of time" for a murder case. David told me that as far as the rapes were concerned, he never thought about the victims until they were there. He said if victims were present, he saw them, he thought about rape, then he performed the rape. This seems to be a fair description of the sexual assault that occurs in robbery cases.

Sexual assault is a rarity in contract killings, even when there is prolonged interaction. Here is a key difference between robbery and sex killers on the one hand, and contract killers on the other. The contract killer likes to have control of the situation. He finds that there is enough unpredictability in the situation itself without creating more. With sex acts, the performers are vulnerable. It is perhaps this flirting with vulnerability that distinguishes robbers and allows them to increase their own risk by engaging in sex acts. Einstadter (1974) has pointed out that risk is probably an additional factor which entices people into robbery situations. He compares this risk-taking with stress-seeking in sport and recreational activities. He notes: "The pitting of the self against calculated odds and overcoming the obstacle, the actual seeking out of a risk condition to test one's abilities, to prove one's worth, is involved in robbery" (Einstadter, 1974:20-21). David acknowledges this need to seek risks in his description of the situation as "addicting."

Another consideration is that the robber is playing with the power that the use of force and the threat of death carries. Short of death, robbers may use various ways to terrorize victims. The recognition of the self as a killer may be sufficient for the contract killer. Joey says, "I like having the power of knowing that I am it, that I can make the final decision of whether someone lives or dies. It is an awesome power" (Fisher, 1975:82). In most cases, the robber is making decisions whether to rape or to kill in the context of each situation. He is much more vulnerable to the suggestions of his group. He may pull the trigger in response to the insistent voice of one of his companions saying, "Shoot him, shoot him." The hit man knows ahead of time that he is going to kill. He deliberately stifles his responses to his victims.

Two final cases will illustrate sexual assault in robbery homicide groups. In the first case, two men were committing a series of robberies at Roman Catholic churches. The robberies began early in July, when Chester asked Andy if he wanted to go with him on a holdup.

Chester said he figured they could get eight or nine thousand dollars. They went to the first church about 10 o'clock. Chester gave Andy a .25 caliber revolver and took a .22 auto rifle himself. They went to the rectory and when the priest answered the door they rushed him and Chester fired one shot. The priest raised his hands and said, "Take anything you want." Chester said, "Where is the safe?" The priest went in the closet and Chester said, "Open the safe or I'll blow your head off." The priest told him he didn't know the combination. They forced him to crawl up the stairs. Just then Andy's gun fired accidently. The priest said, "Please go." Chester hit him on the head with the rifle, then told Andy to tie him up. They left with about $2,000. They tried another church the next week but when they tried to rush the door the night chain was on. The following night they tried another church. This time they found one of the nuns. They tried to make her open the safe. Andy hit her and said, "Open that safe, bitch." Chester pushed her pajamas aside and fondled her legs. He put his fingers in her vagina and rectum. They tried to put her in a closet after that. In the following days they robbed two other churches. The last one they attempted Andy rang the bell while Chester stood by the door. An old priest answered and Andy said he wanted to talk to him. The priest opened the screen and Andy and Chester rushed in. "Take us to the safe," Chester said. The priest said,

"There's no money here." Chester repeated, "Take us to the safe." The priest turned and grabbed Chester and Chester shot. As they started to struggle, Andy ran out to the car. Chester came out, then as they left he told Andy, "I capped him."

These two men had interactions with a number of priests, housekeepers and other parish personnel. They assaulted one priest, killed another, and sexually assaulted one nun. In each case, their actions were in response to another group member and the victims.

The final case involves a 15-year-old boy and a 17-year-old arrested for murder late in 1977. The police record of the 15-year-old began with a B & E when he was nine years old. In the years that followed he had contact with the police for at least 30 crimes ranging from murder to car theft. Both personal and property crimes were included, and early in 1974 he was arrested for a crime very similar to the one we now describe. At 15, Wade's criminal career was well established. His crime partner, Milo, describes the homicide.

Last Monday at around 6 o'clock I went over on the next street to see a friend of mine named Wade. I talked to his sister and she told me he wasn't home. I went over to my cousin's house across the street and was drinking a beer I had with me on his front porch. About 7:15 I saw Wade and called him over. Wade had some money so we went over to the beer store a couple blocks away and bought some wine and beer. We came back and started drinking the stuff and we ended up in the clubhouse in back of my cousin's house. There was my girlfriend and her sister, my cousin, another guy and girl from the neighborhood, Wade and myself. Around midnight everyone had gone home but me and Wade. Wade asked me if I wanted to make some money and I said, "Sure." He said that we would break into old lady Sophie's house who just lived a couple doors away from Wade. I said, "Let's go." We went around to the back of old lady Sophie's house. Wade had a screwdriver and he popped the corner of the window in the rear door and took out a couple pieces of glass and laid them on the grass. He reached in and unlocked the door and we both went inside. We walked up a couple steps and opened a door that was closed. The door let us into the kitchen. All the lights in the house were off but we could still see from the lights outside. Wade was leading and I was following him. We walked through the kitchen, through the dining room and into the living room where the old lady was lying on a couch. Wade grabbed her arms and dragged her into a bedroom located toward the back of the house. He threw her down on the bed and started to screw her. I told him he was a crazy motherfucker to be doing that because we came to get some money and here he was getting laid. After I saw him start screwing her, I walked out of the bedroom and waited til he got done. He took about five minutes. During that time I heard a smack. When Wade brought her out of the bedroom I noticed her nose was bleeding a lot. I pulled a chair out of the dining room and Wade set her down. I held her down in the chair and Wade tied her hands and feet to the chair with some sheets he got somewhere. Wade cut some cords off lamps with his knife that he had in his pocket and tied her some more. I took a knife and cut the phone wires. Wade asked her where the money was. She said, "In the bank." He slapped her in the face with the back of his hand. Then he started looking around the house for money. I sat down on the floor next to the lady. Wade gave me a plastic bag and when he would find some money in different areas of the house I would put the money in the bag. Every so often Wade would ask the lady where the money was and hit her in the face. I guess we were in the house about thirty to forty-five minutes. Right toward the end the lady told us that the money was under a rug in the parlor. We didn't know what the parlor was so we didn't find it. We started to leave and Wade put a sheet over the lady's head. She was sort of moaning and moving around. We left the same way we came in. We got in the car and Wade started it with the same old screwdriver he used to break into the house. Wade drove to our old neighborhood and we cut up the money that we got from the house. I got about $125 in bills and change as my share and Wade got about the same. We left some change to split later. We went to his house but he couldn't get in. I went to my girlfriend's and went to sleep. The clothes that I had on had got some blood on them so I put them in a plastic bag and threw them away near the park.

In spite of the fact that the woman was 83 years old, neither Wade nor Milo had any real reservations about the rape. Milo made a mild comment, but made no effort to prevent the rape nor any other assault of the victim. In cases where the group members have equal status, they will sometimes attempt to dissuade other members from assault or rape of a victim if they disapprove by telling them to stop, or saying "let's go." Some group members check out the responses of the others in the group by saying, "Let's rape her" or "we should kill them" and proceed only if the others support the suggestion. Group leaders often take the acquiesence of the other group members for granted. There is some indication, from the lack of response of group members to sexual assault, that it is not considered too serious. It is rarely important enough for group members to argue over.

SUMMARY

Homicides in which sex is the primary motive are rarer than sexual assaults or other types of felony homicide. The fact that these cases rarely involve a gun probably proves this in part. The victims are also less often armed. This is further proof that the killings are rarely physically defensive responses. Probably one of the major reasons for killing in sexual assault cases is the fear that the assault will be reported and the offender will be unable to escape the repercussions.

Homicides in which sexual assaults occur appear to fall into two major categories: first, those in which the sexual assault is the primary motive and in which the homicide occurs due to defensive, malefic, or future defensive definitions of the situation on the part of the killer; second, cases in which the sexual assault is a part of the interaction. The victim of the assault or a witness in the interaction is killed for reasons essentially unrelated to the sexual behavior. The victims appear to be depersonalized, as in other felony homicides, and the killers have little concern for them.

PART THREE

Part Three examines some of the patterns in homicides, within the homicide group and between killers and victims. Also considered are career contingencies and several alternate paths to developing killer role identities.

7 Patterns in Felony Homicides

In this chapter the common interaction patterns between killers and victims, as well as those within the killer groups, are considered. Earlier chapters have shown that homicides often involve many more persons than just a shooter and victim. The stages of the homicide interaction, both with and without the victims present, have been shown. It is clear that there is great variation in the amount of time in which the victims and the killers are together.

The length of the interaction varies. There can be less than a minute in street executions involving little or no verbal interaction between killers and victims. In other cases, victims and killers may spend hours together. The police rarely attempt to elicit complete records of conversations from arrested killers or witnesses. Some reports, however, are surprisingly detailed. Some detectives do seem to elicit more complete and descriptive material.

THE CONDUCT OF VICTIMS

In many of these cases, as has been suggested earlier, the decision to kill the victim has been made prior to the encounter. The actions of the victims during the homicide interaction are constantly being evaluated. It is difficult to predict even what known victims will do in a situation of such extreme stress. Killers and victims make constant judgments throughout the interaction in an attempt to predict outcomes.

BEGGING

Begging is a technique commonly used by people who are threatened and spared. That it occurs regardless of the outcome of the crime suggests that it is not sufficient either to cause or prevent murder. In some cases, the victim does seem to strike a chord that appeals to values of certain killers. One might speculate that begging appeals to the killer's sense of power over life and death and he might therefore decide to let some potential victims live.

"Man, please don't kill me. I don't know nothin' about this, man. Please, please, don't kill me."

"Please don't do this to me. Why you doing this to me? I don't even know you that good."

More experienced killers do not listen to the victims. They recognize their own vulnerability. Ricardo mentions that learning to ignore the victims' pleas was part of his training. Others, however, tend to be annoyed by begging. One wounded survivor described his understanding of the killer's actions, pointing out: "They shot James because he wouldn't shut up. They didn't kill Ann because she had children." Both the on-the-spot decision-making and the different responses to victims are illustrated in this single case.

STOICISM

Refusing to cry out or beg, and other demonstrations of bravery, may win the admiration of members of the killer group. It also provides them with expectations of retaliation from the person if he or she were to be left alive. Victims who appear not to be afraid are considered to be foolish, unstable, and thus unpredictable. The person who suffers tortures bravely is respected but considered dangerous. David mentioned that he respected one of the victims and his conduct; however, the murder still took place.

BRIBERY, BARGAINING, COOPERATION

Many victims will offer money or some other form of reward for being left unharmed. They will tell where money or weapons are hidden to demonstrate good faith. If it is a robbery situation, the killers will play along until they think they have all the valuables. In a contract situation, they will either accept the bribes or point out that the contract has already been taken. In any case, they will usually not spare the victim as a result of bargaining. Ricardo pointed out: "I'm gonna kill them because I got everything they got anyhow." Joey (Fisher, 1974) however, considered it beneath his dignity to rob. The responses also depend on whether it is a contract, a robbery or a revenge murder.

"Please don't shoot me, I won't tell anyone."

"No, no, wait, wait. I got stuff at my momma's house. I'll get you money."

"Don't kill me. I'll leave town."

"Don't hurt my wife. She's sick."
"My wife's sick. Can she put the baby down?"

"I don't have it, but I'll get it in the morning when the bank is open."

"Don't shoot me. I'm a friend. Our families know each other. I don't care what you do."

"Wait a minute. Let's talk this over. If it's money you want, it's in the front drawer."

SCREAMING, CALLING FOR HELP

Screaming or calling for help almost always precipitates action by the perpetrators. The perpetrators become apprehensive that someone will come or call the police, and the loudness and noise irritate the already tense offenders. They want nothing more than to shut the victim up. This desire to shut the victim up is particularly true in sex murders, but also in robbery homicides. Screaming for help on the street is likely to cause a robber or a rapist to abandon the crime, but the victim is likely to be wounded or killed.

"They shot me. Call my father."

Victim: "Help me."
Witness: "I can't, I'm scared. But I'll call the police."

"Get me to the hospital."

"Help, police! Help, somebody! Please help me. Help, police! They robbed me."

The offenders are likely to respond by telling the victims to shut up, gagging them, or using some other form of violence.

CHALLENGE, HOSTILITY, ARGUMENT, CONTEMPT

David says:

When people are being robbed they should do exactly what the man with the gun says. Some people, they get an attitude. Now me, if somebody had a gun on me I'd do anything they say, maybe even a little bit more. I'd go farther than a lot of those people do.

Many people argue with or challenge armed felons. We have no way of knowing how many times this frightens them away or the number of times that the perpetrators feel that they must respond with violence. There are certainly many more robbery homicides than there are justifiable homicides by intended victims. Criminals themselves admit that the victim's lack of recognition of their "authority" puts them in a position where they feel required to use force to establish their dominance.

Block (1977:71) has mentioned that resistance will often prevent robbery completion. Other studies (Feeney and Weir, 1975; Conklin, 1972) have shown, however, that it is more likely to cause injury.

Two men walked into a small market run by a man and his sister. One pointed a sawed-off .410 shotgun at the store owner. The owner said, "You're kidding." The man shot. He then pointed the gun at the sister and turned and they both ran out of the store.

Some armed robbers say that they use violence, loudness of commands and swearing at the beginning of a robbery to immediately establish their authority (Miller, 1978). Many times they will give orders but not allow sufficient time for their orders to be carried out before they hit or shove their victims. David also mentions acting mean at the beginning of the interaction. Perhaps they feel that any reluctance to use force may be perceived by victims as a cue to challenge them. Any question of willingness to use force must be responded to immediately. Many victims, however, even when they are armed, are somewhat unwilling to use enough force to overcome the criminals. Therefore, it is usually an uneven encounter, even when the victim apparently has the advantage. Some victims will even say to the killers, "Go ahead. Shoot." The killers usually do. Following are a series of victim statements that express contempt or challenge.

Victim: "I'm not scared. I've got a gun too."

Killer: "I'm gonna tie you up 'til we decide what to do with you."
Victim: "I'm not gonna let you."

Killer: "Man, give the money up."
Victim: "Man, I'm not givin' you the bag."

Three men discussed robbing an acquaintance who they heard had just received some money. They picked up two others and decided how they would split the money. They loitered around until dark, then three of them went in the house. They knocked the victim down. One of them kept the victim at gunpoint then began hitting him with the gun. Two other people who were there were ordered to lie on the floor. The victim was being beaten but he continued to resist. He told the man with the gun, "I'll make you use that gun." He shot the victim, they robbed him and ran out.

"Aw, baby, you don't know what you're doing."

In each of these situations the victim rejected the role identity of killer presented by the perpetrator, and in each of these cases the victim was shot.

The last example again typifies the action when a victim challenges the authority of the killer. By the victim's refusal to accept the identity that the killer is presenting, the killer is placed in a position where he must take action if he is to substantiate the identity. In those cases where the identity being presented is that of a robber, there is the option of assaulting the victim or leaving the scene. It would appear that in many cases of armed robbery, the identity being presented is ambiguous. Challenge or the refusal to cooperate is one way in which the killers identity may become clarified to the victim's disadvantage. If the killer has hypothesized a killer role identity, he may have rehearsed responses to a victim who refuses to respond to him in this identity. Or, the killer may have indicated to his crime partners a willingness to assume this role and thus may feel that refusal to respond to the victim's challenge will result in the loss of identity within the crime group.

In another case the victim, and some friends, were having a birthday party. The defendant was loud. He bragged that he belonged to an outlaw motorcycle club and that he had a gun. The victim asked him to leave.

The defendant said being a member of an outlaw club gave him the right to carry a gun and that he knew how to use it. He pulled the gun and said: "This will keep me here." The victim said: "If you're going to shoot me, go ahead."

CONNING, MANIPULATION, ESCAPE

Conning, manipulation and escape have some potential as techniques for avoiding murder. But, as has been mentioned before, since felony murders often involve groups, using them becomes more difficult. The decision to kill that is made on the spot, as is often the case in sex and robbery homicides, does not have the commitment that the contract killing does. In robbery murders, members of the group are more likely to make the decisions independently. In some robberies, especially those that occur in private homes, the group members may split up. Thus, there may be various confrontations going on in different parts of the house. In most cases, when there is a robbery in the home, the robbers will attempt to bring all persons in the house together. In this way, the victims can be guarded or tied by one person and the other members of the group are free to roam through the house looking for loot.

In some situations, when houses are broken into at night, there are some members of the household either sleeping, or scattered throughout the house. The robber group will take these people with them to ascertain where money or valuables are kept. Some victims talk and attempt to establish a relationship with individual robbers. A relationship, or the arousal of sympathy, may cause that member to speak up for the victim. Victims attempt to edge away from the group, move toward the door or in other ways make an effort to escape. If they move slowly, and do not startle the persons with weapons, they will usually be sent back or beaten if they are noticed. Any kind of fast, abrupt or violent moves, particularly in the direction of any robbers, will usually result in shooting. Escape attempts that do not frighten or startle people do not usually result in dangerous outcomes. Victims who escape usually do so by running out a door, or throwing themselves out of windows. Often injury results, but it usually is not critical. Those who run may be shot and wounded but successfully escape. Others survive by playing dead. The vic-

tims who make escape attempts have usually arrived at
the conclusion that they are going to be killed. Those
who feel they have a chance to survive by going along
with the robbers do not make escape attempts. Victims
who are able to avoid panic are constantly assessing and
reassessing their chances of survival instead of using
cooperative, threatening, manipulative or escape behavior. Some victims attempt to manipulate robbers by cast-
ing doubts on their companions, or by attempting to
show them how it would be to their benefit to help the
intended victim. Others manipulate by suggesting that
they don't care about the material things or others in the
house but will just be happy to survive. Under no circumstances, they claim, would they go to the police.
These tactics are rarely effective.

David described one case in which a female victim
told such a sad story that one of the group members felt
sorry for her. He wanted to go and kill her errant husband if the husband didn't treat her better. A witness
describes a situation in which she took advantage of the
victim's confrontation with the group to hide.

> Two couples were staying in the same motel. After
> they had been there for about two months the de-
> fendant's motel room was broken into and a large
> amount of cash as well as some other things were
> taken. The next day he went down to the victim's
> room and asked him to come down to his room.
> When he got there the defendant's brother and
> another man were waiting. They accused him of
> breaking into the room. He denied that he had done
> it and invited them down to his room to look for the
> missing items. His cohab let them in. All three men
> had guns in their hands. They told the couple to lay

down on the floor. They asked the victim where his
gun was. He said he didn't have a gun but his
girlfriend told them there was a gun under the blan-
ket. One of the men took some money from a box
and put it in his pocket. They told the couple to
stand up but not to try to run. Some friends of the
victim came to the room just as they were leaving.
They saw the defendants with their drawn guns.
The victim shouted, "If you are going to do anything to me, you are going to do it here." He
pounded on a motel door and shouted. The woman
ducked behind a couch and heard two shots.

ATTACK, PHYSICAL CONTACT WITH KILLERS

The victim, a 77-year-old white man, left the
cleaners and was walking toward his car. Two
black teenage boys approached him and demanded
his money. The victim refused and grabbed the arm
of one boy and the other shot him.

Physically counter-attacking someone who is intent
on robbing, raping or killing a victim usually results in
immediate, and violent retaliation. Criminals generally
operate within the rules of the violent subculture. They
thus respond to violence with a show of greater force.
The criminals want to complete their crime without being hurt themselves. They tend to be annoyed if the
victim attempts to take control in any way or refuses to
accept the identity the killers are presenting or their
definition of the situation.

DENIAL, REPENTANCE

Some victims attempt to sway the killers by denying that
they have ever injured the attackers, their bosses, or any

one related to them. If they have themselves been involved, or are thought to have been involved in rip-offs,
killings, or altercations, they will often declare their
repentance and promise to make reparations and not to
repeat their offense.

"Man, I fucked up some of the drugs."

"It was Thomas who crossed you, not me."

Although the victim may be telling the truth, and even
sometimes convince the killers, it is often too late once
the encounter has been initiated. In punishment situations, the killers usually only kill the person who is
considered responsible. In torture situations, where witnesses are present when the killers attempt to extract
information or admissions from victims, there is always
the problem of what, if any, action will be taken toward
witnesses. In cases where the witnesses have viewed the
willingness of the killers to torture and kill, even if they
are left alive, they will rarely appear to testify.

AWARENESS CONTEXTS

The above is naturally not an exhaustive list of all victim
behaviors. It does attempt to cover those patterns of
conduct which are most frequent. Unless the victims are
expected to reveal some kind of information, once the
homicide encounter has been initiated victims are usually expected to keep quiet until the killers leave. Victims may perceive their best strategy to be to try to
establish a good relationship with the killers or to establish a sympathetic identity for themselves. They may
decide that absolute cooperation, or not drawing attention to themselves, will give them the best chance of
survival.

The victims in homicides try to attribute some kind of motivation and identity to the killers to help them decide how they should act. They attempt to assess whether the killer wants to rob, rape, torture or kill them. They try to elicit information without antagonizing the killers. They rarely are allowed any interaction with other victims, as the killers view this interaction with suspicion. The killers do their best to maintain fear, without revealing whether or not they intend to murder the victims. They want the victims to continue to cooperate in the hope that their lives will be spared. Both victims and criminals are constantly trying to figure out the best course of action. They try to predict what the others will do in a situation which is dangerous to all parties.

As was mentioned by Joey (Fisher, 1975), the victim may accurately assess the killer's role identity and intent but then reject this knowledge. Glaser and Strauss (1964) suggested that the assessment of the participants in the crime occurs within awareness contexts that are open in varying degrees. In some situations the killer may be aware of having a killer identity, but conceal it from the victim. In other situations, the killer identity may be secondary to that of robber or rapist. However, even when the victim is suspicious of the killer's identity, both victims and killers may cooperate in a pretense that confirms or denies the identity.

Killers, when discussing the crime situations and the responses of the victims, frequently comment on the fact that they concealed their intention from the victim. Or the victim may have attributed a different identity to them from the one they actually had. Victims who escape often explain their escape in terms of having correctly determined the killer's identity.

CONDUCT PATTERNS OF THE KILLER GROUP
TOWARD VICTIMS

The conduct patterns of killer groups depend greatly on whether or not they are going to use deception or fear as a means of manipulating the victims. In a great number of cases, a certain amount of deception is used, at least until the killers know their positions. Even in street encounters, if groups intend to rob, rape or kill, they conceal their wishes until they are close to the victims. If they use deception there will generally be some type of reason offered by a group member for being admitted into a building, or part of the building. Any group member(s) who gains admittance will try not to arouse suspicion. If they enter a store, tavern or restaurant, they usually take on the role of customers. In gaining entrance to a residence, they either have an acquaintance with the resident, or they ask to use the phone or invent some other excuse. Women frequently are used to gain entry because they do not arouse much suspicion. However, gaining entry to a private home is difficult, as people tend to be unwilling to let strangers into the house. Frequently, no deception is employed. The door is simply stormed and forced.

PRONOUNCEMENTS

The pronouncement is a standard opening for robbery homicides. But it is rarely used in crimes such as executions or rapes. There, the situation is kept ambiguous for as long as possible. In robberies, however, by defining the situation as a "holdup" or "stickup," the group draws attention to the weapon and implies that the intention is not to kill, but to take money or property.

"This is a holdup," or "This is a stickup," is the usual

opening statement. Occasionally in a contract killing the hit man will say, "This is it."

COMMANDS

"Freeze." "Don't move." "Lay on the floor." "Put your hands on your head." Contract hits do not usually begin with pronouncements, but often a command will be used when the killer brings out his or her weapon. The deception is at an end and a redefinition of the situation made, and the victims attribute different identities to the killers. The initial command was an effect much like that of the pronouncement, but it does not clearly define the situation to the victims and only serves to indicate that they are in danger. If it is not a quick hit, or, as often is the case, where there is no conversation at all, the initial statement is likely to be a command. Commands are a continual part of the interaction between killers and victims and also among the offender group members. Victims respond by obeying the commands, refusing to obey, or by disregarding them. As was pointed out earlier, the killers are likely to take action if the commands are refused. In the initial stages of the interaction, they will respond quickly if commands are ignored. Once the killers are satisfied that they have control of the situation, they seem to be more willing to allow sufficient time for commands to be obeyed. They will often repeat them without using force or taking punitive action.

IDENTIFICATION OR VERIFICATION OF VICTIM

"Hey, Joe." "Are you John Smith?" "Which one of you is Sam Jones?" Or an identification can be: "Is that Gary Jones?" In execution killings, it is sometimes necessary to make sure that the intended victim is the one the killers think he is. This type of verification especially occurs when the hit is being done at the victim's home or hang-out and victims are responding at the door. Since the killers may shoot through a closed, or only partially opened, door, they may not even see the victim. In other cases, verification announces that the killing is an execution.

DECLARATION OF INTENT

The declaration of intent serves to clarify the situation for victims and witnesses. In some situations, statements such as "we're going to take all the money" are redundant or simply reemphasize and further clarify. In cases such as the one described below, the intent is couched in terms of animosity. It differentiates the victim from the other persons, and serves to let the others know that the intent to kill is reserved for the particular victim.

> A group of men and a woman were sitting around in a narcotics pad drinking wine. Two of the men left and came back in in half an hour with a case. One of them took a sawed-off shotgun out of the case, put it together, and pointed it at the victim who was the owner of the pad. He said, "Give it up." The victim put a lot of money and narcotics from his pockets on the floor in front of him. The man with the shotgun walked up to him and placed the gun against his chest. He said, "I've been waiting three years for this." Both men then told the others, "Forget what you saw here and you won't get hurt," and left.

Intent to rob may be announced at the beginning of a robbery homicide, but intent to kill is usually declared only at the point at which the killer is ready to kill. In most robbery homicides, or contract killings that are not quick hits, or where the victims are going to be taken to another location to be killed, the killers deny that they intend to kill the victim.

REASSURANCE

"Nobody's gonna get hurt." "Do what you're told and we won't hurt you." "We just want to talk to Jesse James." In the following cases, the killer could rationalize the killing of the victim who had previously announced that he was not going to cooperate. However, one criminal apparently defined the situation differently from the others. The first criminal was willing to negotiate with the victim, while the second considered the victim's refusal to negotiate as an indication that he might resist or be reaching for a weapon. While the first criminal responded to the denial of his identity with statements designed to threaten the victim, he responded to the witness reassuring him that he would not be harmed.

> In an armed robbery of a Coney Island [name of a restaurant] three men came into the restaurant while the fourth man stayed in the car. One man remained at the front of the restaurant while two others bought a coke. One started to walk toward the back of the restaurant, the other announced that it was a holdup, and both of them drew revolvers. The victim said, "I'm not giving you any money." The one who had announced that it was a hold up said, "We're not fooling, Mr. Jones, we're for real." He repeated this several times. The victim reached under the counter and as he turned, the man by the

door fired at his back. The second man walked around and took a bag with money in it. The first man asked a customer, "Do you have any money?" The customer said, "No." The man said, "Then don't worry, we're not going to hurt you." Then all three ran out of the store.

A defendant went to the home of the victim and his wife. He sat and talked to them for about a half hour. He drew a gun then and told the victim and his wife that he wanted all their money. The victim gave him his wallet. His wife took $30 from her purse. The defendant then asked them for some rope to tie them up. He said, "I just want to tie you so I can get away. I won't hurt you." He took them to the basement and made them take off their outer clothes. He then shot a number of times hitting the victim in the head and wounding the wife in the head and arm. A friend found them and called the police.

Henry, Ricardo, and David all considered it important to establish some kind of rapport with their victims. They found that if they could lull their victims into a false security and trust, they could carry out the crimes more easily. They often received an additional reward for their courtesy to victims—the victims volunteered information to them. David mentioned that some members of his group were continually "mean" throughout the encounter. But after the initial stages, when the group had established control, he would adopt behavior designed to establish trust and liking. Ricardo also commented on the feeling of trust that his pleasing manner established in his victims.

SWEARING

Swearing is common lingo for robbers. It is used mainly to show toughness and to frighten victims into submission. It is used to control, dominate and demoralize. Although swearing is common in street language, it can be added to, or removed from, the vocabulary at will. This can be seen in criminal interactions with police, or in the courtroom. The most common depersonalizing words are referring to women as "bitch" or "cunt" and men or mixed groups as "motherfucker."

A small group of parishioners were sitting in a Roman Catholic church waiting for mass to begin. An usher started down the middle aisle. Two men jumped up with revolvers. One of them grabbed the usher and put his arms behind him and started pushing him down the aisle toward the altar. He said, "Come on, motherfucker, give me your money." He started slapping the usher so the usher tried to grab him. He shot, and when the usher fell, he shot twice more and then ripped his pocket and took his wallet.

SHOUTING

As with swearing, shouting is used as a dominance tactic and is common at least in initial phases of an encounter, or in murder situations where the killers are trying to extract information.

THREATS, PROMISES

Use of threats is common and particularly with reference to the use of weapons. "Don't move or I'll blow your head off." "Give me your wallet or I'll cut you." "Show me where the money is or I'll kill your ol' lady." These are often followed by some expression of force or promises. "You won't be hurt if you'll just show us where the money/dope/jewelry is."

In a 1973 case in which a two-year-old child was killed, a threat was made and disregarded by her father.

Two men and two women came to the father's house. One of the men came in to sell the father some drugs and asked if his friend could come in. They talked about the drugs and sat around a dining room table with both the father and the visitors using various kinds of drugs. After remaining in the house for several hours, one of the defendants asked the father if he had anything that would clean paint off his shoe. He was told that there was some gasoline that had been used to clean paintbrushes in the bathroom. He went in and returned from the bathroom with a bottle. He grabbed the baby and asked the father if it was gasoline. The father said, "Yes, hey, what goin' on?" The defendant said, "Do what I say or I'll kill her" and poured the gasoline over the baby's head. She started to cry and rubbed her eyes. He pulled out a knife and a rope and told the other man who had come with him to tie the father up. His partner didn't move. The father grabbed his daughter from the man and threw her in the corner. He turned a table over between the man and his daughter and they started fighting in front of the little girl. The defendant lit a match and, although the father tried to hit him with a chair, he managed to throw it on the little girl who burst into flames. The father grabbed his baby and tried to put out the fire. The two women ran out of the house. The father finally extinguished the flames in the bathtub, but the baby died.

VIOLENCE, PHYSICAL FORCE

Knocking over furniture, or smashing inanimate objects are tactics used to terrorize and control victims. Many groups use force at the start of an encounter to establish authority. Pushing people down, hitting them with gun butts—any kind of violent behavior—is usually like the swearing and threats. They are intended to dominate and demoralize. Occasionally, someone will shoot into the floor or the air. Such shooting is rare because while shouting and loud noises may be ignored, gunshots will often result in the police being called. Some groups do not shoot until the end of a crime, or leave immediately after shots are fired, even if they have not completed what they are doing.

QUESTIONS, REQUESTS, ENCOURAGEMENT

"Are there any guns here?" "Where is Jack Lincoln?" "Who else is in the house?" "Please, empty out your pockets." These questions may be put to the victims politely or not, depending on the crime group and the individual criminal. The encouragement usually takes the form of: "That's right, just keep on sitting there quietly." "O.K. You're doing just fine, not causing any trouble."

Two men and a woman came to the victim's door. The woman went up on the porch and knocked. She called to him, "Lewis, let me in." She called the men up on the porch with her and said, "Lewis, let us in or we'll kick the door in." Lewis and his two children ran upstairs as they kicked the door in. Lewis grabbed an iron pipe. One of the men had a .38 revolver. He said, "Halt!" Lewis came down the stairs with his hands up. The man said, "Where is the money?" Lewis replied, "I don't have any." The man kept asking for the money. Finally he asked Lewis, "Do you want me to kill you?" Lewis said, "No." The children heard four shots and the three defendants ran from the house.

The victim was in his house with two friends when the defendants came in. One defendant grabbed a shotgun and pointed it at the victim and said, "Why did you do that?" The victim said, "I haven't done anything, man; I didn't set you up!" He shot the victim in the chest. They took some drugs from the victim and told one of his friends to call an ambulance and they left the house.

RIDICULE, EXPRESSION OF CONTEMPT

As a form of ridicule, reference may be made to bodily characteristics, such as fatness, or behavior that shows fear. Often these belittling statements are addressed to other group members in the victim's presence.

In one case, in which two middle-aged sisters were assaulted and their father killed, the grimness of the case was lightened momentarily for the police during one sister's account of the interaction. She reported to the police, barely repressing her satisfaction, that one of the killers repeatedly referred to her sister as "that fat bitch."

In accounts of killings by both killers and witnesses, victims are often referred to by physical characteristics, even when their names are known. Henry, in describing how one of his multiple killings went down, referred to his victims as "the one with the nice shape" and "the one with the glasses." Although Henry was aware of the victim's names even prior to the killing, he used this tactic to keep the killings as impersonal as possible. It is quite common for the killers to use this tactic even though they may have known the victims' names.

CHALLENGE

"Go ahead and try something." "You think you can make it to the door?" "What are you going to do now, big man?"

Two men and two women entered an A & P store. One man remained in the front of the store while the others shopped. When the shoppers got to the front of the store both men pulled guns and said, "This is a holdup. Don't move." One of the men took the cash from the cash register. They started shouting and everyone dropped to the floor. The man at the front of the store said to the security guard, "Run, motherfucker, run!" He started to run and was shot in the leg. The man at the register started to run for the front door and was shot twice in the head. The cashier was also shot in the head but the bullet only grazed her head. They all ran from the store.

APOLOGY, REGRET

"Sorry we have to do this." "Too bad you didn't take care of your business."

A young girl, who knew one of the house resident's sons, asked the victim if she could come in to call a cab. After she got in she took a .25 caliber automatic out of her purse, pointed it and said, "I'm sorry that I have to do this but if I don't let that man in here, they will kill my baby."

EXPLANATION

"This has to be done" or "This is a contract."

> In a case where two men were killed in a narcotics pad, seven were sitting around the dining room and the common-law wife of one of the victims, whose apartment it was, was in the bedroom. The doorman called his brother, one of the defendants, aside. A second defendant said, "You are the one" and began shooting. One victim tried to escape and was shot. Two other men threw themselves on the floor; one was wounded and the other was shot four times. The defendant, who was talking to his brother, entered the bedroom where the victim's common-law wife was and demanded money and narcotics from her. She asked, "Why did you kill them?" He replied, "I was told your old man was going to kill me."

Killers, like other people, vary in how much explanation they supply for their actions. Occasionally they are under instruction to make sure that their victims know who is responsible for their murder, or to point out to the victims that their death was brought on by their own actions. In most cases, however, explanation only reflects the killer's need to verbalize his own rationalizations, perhaps for his own benefit and perhaps for his companions.

SELF-REFERENCE

"We are junkies" or "I don't fool around." This type of self-reference serves to identify the killer, and is a form of threat. It is, in effect, the same as saying, "I'll blow your head off." In one case a killer announced his identity by saying, "I am a professional dirty mother-fucker!" Such self-references are often used, as is swearing and shouting, to increase fear in the victims. In the shared perspective of the killers and victims the statement, "We are junkies," means "We are desperate, dangerous and unpredictable." The same effect may be obtained by oblique references to recent highly publicized cases. They indicate that the killers had some involvement with them, and serve to further intimidate the victims.

RESTRAINT, TORTURE

Torture involves close contact between the victims and killers. Usually tying is done with articles at hand. Appliance cords are cut off on the spot; so is clothing such as pantyhose and scarves. Very rarely are binding items brought in, although occasionally tape is carried in. Torture items are also picked up at the site, usually such items as cigarettes, matches, knives, forks, broomsticks, curtain rods and the like.

Most torture cases are revenge or gangland killings. But torture is sometimes used to secure cooperation from the victims or to get information about where their money or goods may be hidden. Torture, unlike using force to gain control of the situation, does not appear to be a standard pattern in felony homicides. The use of torture or sexual assault seems more to reflect the proclivities of the killers rather than task-related behavior necessary for completion of the crime. In a few cases, use of torture is part of the instructions given to the killers by contractors. Organized crime cases, for example, use torture in cases of defecting members. They hold them up as an example lest others consider violating some of the mob rules.

A friend drove the victim to his house and went in with him. About fifteen minutes after they got there a man from the apartment above came and asked them to come upstairs. They went in the room where there were two other men and two women. All four of them pulled guns. One of them said, "You fucked up and you are going to die." They tied and gagged the victim and his friend and told them both to lie on the floor. The victim wouldn't do it. They beat him with their guns and one of them stabbed him. The friend freed his hands, which were tied with an electric cord, and ran. They fired ten or fifteen shots at him but he escaped and called the police. The victim was found later in a burning car. His hands were still tied and he had been shot in the head.

The victim, a 37-year-old black woman, was in an apartment with three other women and three men. She was given some wine and drugs and later she said she was going to leave. One of the men said, "You're not going anyplace." She tried to jump out the apartment window but was pulled back by one of the women. Another man was called on the phone while the victim was held by two of the women. They all went across the hall. Three of the men beat her with their hands. She was then bound and gagged by one of the women. Two of the women heated a kitchen knife and took turns burning the victim on her legs and lower body. All of them then beat her and burnt her with cigarettes. Finally, after many hours of this, she was taken to a car by three of the men. They returned an hour later. The victim was found the next day behind an abandoned building. In addition to the earlier tortures, she had been strangled and shot many times.

SEXUAL REFERENCES, SEX

Sexual abuse includes touching or fondling breasts, buttocks, or genitals, exposing genitals, rape, sodomy, oral-genital sex and such statements as, "I should rape you."

Four 19-year-old men went to the house of an old couple. Two went to the front door and one to the side while the fourth remained in the car. They began banging on the doors and the two at the front forced their way in. They had tire irons, a nightstick and a revolver as weapons. They forced the 80-year-old woman into a back room and raped and beat her. Two of them beat her husband into unconsciousness. They then ransacked the house, taking money and jewelry. The woman died but the man recovered.

Sexual offenses are common in homicide cases and are discussed in detail in chapter 6.

CONDUCT BETWEEN GROUP MEMBERS AT HOMICIDE SCENE

GIVING ORDERS

"Stay by the door." "Watch them." "Get their money." These orders do not necessarily reflect commands from leaders to followers. Often, however, certain group members repeatedly take over during the confrontation.

Two men and a woman disarmed three drug dealers that they were visiting. They tied two men

*in the front room and one other in a bedroom. The
woman told one of her companions, "Off all of
them. I don't want no shit behind this." The man
said, "O.K., baby," and shot the two men in the
head. The other man shot the man in the bedroom
and they all left.*

The order to shoot appears frequently in accounts of
killings, both by witnesses and killers. It seems to be
most influential in situations where there is a struggle
and the victim is resisting or attempting to escape. In
other situations, as shown in the above account, the
shooting follows a direct order of one of the members to
another. The status of the person giving the order in
these cases is of major importance. That is apparent in
the threat from the victim. Some criminals are only
group, is threatened. In Anthony's words, "It is all about
me then." In other cases, a command to shoot is simply
a confirmation that someone in the group agrees with
the shooter's appraisal of the situation.

QUESTIONS, DIRECTION SEEKING

"Should I tie them up?" "Did you look in that bedroom?" Direction seeking serves a number of purposes
during the homicide. It can be an indication of deference
to a leader or a group member with greater experience in
such situations. In acts that have serious consequences
for the criminals, such as murder, it is also a way for a
group member to share or deny responsibility. In many
cases, where action is not rapid in the killing, the decision to kill or not to kill witnesses is turned over to the
group leader. In groups that have worked together on a

number of crimes, the decision-making process may be well established. Direction seeking continues along the established pattern.

ENCOURAGEMENT

"That's the way to handle them." Encouraging a criminal, particularly in torturing or killing a victim, is quite common. It may be verbal or nonverbal. It seems to happen more often than does discouragement of a group member. Group members often say, "Go ahead, shoot" to another member who has a weapon. They approve and encourage each other in acts against the victim. Donald encourages and thereby hopes to get the other group members involved in the actual killing. David recognized many of Donald's commands, suggestions and encouragements to be manipulative and mentioned that Donald himself often did not participate during homicides. In another case, one criminal was dissatisfied with the performance of another and told him, "Here, give me that gun and I'll show you how to off that motherfucker."

DISCOURAGEMENT, DISAGREEMENT

Several men met at the home of one of their girl-friends. One of them mentioned that his brother-in-law ran a dope pad and had beat him out of some money that he wanted to get back. He said he would get in and he would let the others in. Later he went to his brother-in-law's place and when the four others came he let them in. They all had guns and they told their friend and his brother-in-law to lay on the floor. One of the men took a shotgun that was in the apartment. Just then the victim and another man came in. They were also told to lie on the floor. One of the men was stripped of all his clothes as they searched for money. Forty dollars was taken from the brother-in-law's wallet. The man who had taken the shotgun hit three of the men with the butt of the gun. The victim was told to take his clothes off. The man with the shotgun kept hitting him with the gun. He said, "I'm going to kill you all." He shot the victim in the back of the head and said, "Let's kill them all." The others said, "No," and they left.

The willingness of members of a criminal group to discourage one another from rape, torture or murder depends to a large extent on their interrelationships. David, for example, on several occasions, told other members of his group to stop, that they had done enough. He admitted, however, that he was not willing to confront Donald while they were involved in a double murder and torture. Donald's style was to psych himself up for the homicide that he was involved in. He always had himself ready to verbally attack both fellow group members and victims. David and another group member, LeRoy, both described Donald as mean. LeRoy described an episode with Donald after the group had committed a homicide. LeRoy became upset because Donald got "valiant" with him (threatened him). David considered Donald to be in control of himself and not emotionally involved, in spite of his apparently temperamental behavior. He emphasized, in his description of Donald, that Donald was smart and manipulative, mean but not crazy.

PLANNING, DECISION MAKING

Many times the planning for a crime is done ahead of time but is limited to use of weapons, type of transportation, and method of gaining entry. Beyond these details, it is difficult to predict who will participate. In contract killings or execution-style robberies that take place in a home, often an effort is made to plan. But in most robbery homicides, planning is not done beforehand because it is too unpredictable. Only general outlines are developed. Most planning and decisions are made on the spot. Either conferences or unilateral decisions are made at the scene.

In the following case, one of the female defendants in a crime describes the interactions between two male and two other female defendants and the female victim. She describes the decision making during the crime and the ongoing modification of plans of action.

After we sat around talking with Jean (the female victim) for about one half hour, Beany and Leon grabbed her. They told her that I had a gun. Beany told Leon to go in the kitchen and get something to tie the woman with. After a few minutes Beany sent me in to find out what was taking so long. (Leon knew the woman and pretended he was being robbed too). He told me to go and order Sissy (the other woman) and himself back into the living room. When he came back he put on an act saying to Beany, "Why do you want to do this to me?" Beany told him to tie the woman up. Sissy and I wanted to leave but Leon said, "No, wait." He had a knife in his hand that he kept clapping against his hand. He told Beany, "This isn't going to work. This ain't sharp enough." Jeans said, "Please don't kill me. I'm a person trying to get over just like you are." Leon said, "I'm not going to kill you. Just don't scream." He took her to the bedroom. It sounded like she was screaming with something stuffed in her mouth. He came back out. He had taken off his shirt and jacket and was in his t-shirt looking hot and sweaty. He said to Beany, "I can't do it." They both went into the bedroom then.

The victim operated a blind pig out of his apartment. Customers that night saw four men and a woman they didn't know. One of the men was heard to say, "Well, let's do it if we're going to do it. If anyone else comes in we won't have another chance." There was a brief conversation with the victim and then a shot was heard.

In the first case, the decision to kill the victim was made on the spot by the two men, without consulting their female partners. This is not to say that the women were unaware of the decision, but that it was taken for granted that they would go along with it. Both on-the-spot and planned decision making are common in homicides. The criminal group members may discuss the feasibility of leaving some of the victims alive and may strive for informal agreement at the scene. In some groups there is an attempt to achieve consensus; in others only high status members are given the opportunity to voice agreement or disagreement. In other groups members assume a shared perspective about killing and it is assumed that all will agree on chosen actions. In the planning stage, members are given a chance to voice objections. In cases where there is doubt about a member's ability, he may be encouraged to participate in the actual killing. If one of the group shows too strong an objection during the homicide, and the other members are worried about him holding things up during an investigation, he may be threatened or even killed.

SUMMARY

In chapter 7, patterns of interaction among criminal group members and between killer groups and their victims have been considered. It was pointed out in earlier chapters that there are specific kinds of tasks that are shared in a criminal group committing felony homicides. These tasks include entry to the scene, control of victims and escape, as well as robbing and killing. Common patterns of group interaction can be observed while crimes are performed. Group members share a common perspective concerning their crimes. This perspective, and the way in which the homicide is related, is often similarly held by victims. While recognizing that the crime and situational similarities create some common patterns, we do not imply that the homicide encounter is predictable. In any given homicide, the reality of perception and the motives attributed to the various participants are contingent upon the particular situation. Throughout the homicide, there are negotiations within the killer group itself, between the killers, and between the killers and their victims. Life and death hang in the balance during these interactions. Thus all homicides have high levels of excitement and anxiety. Even the most nonchalant killer is aware that his own life and future is in danger in any of these episodes. Each participant handles the meaning of the fear that this knowledge creates differently, depending on the self concepts of the killers and victims. Kleinke (1978) has suggested that for people who find the admission of fear in a danger situation incongruous with their own self definition, fear may be redefined as sexual arousal. This would help to explain the frequency of sexual assaults upon unlikely targets in these settings.

8 Killer Identities and Career Contingencies

Up to this point this study has focused primarily on crime group activities and homicide interactions. In this chapter we shall turn our attention toward the killer role and how it becomes a part of the criminal's self-concept. We shall examine a second area: the career killer. How are people recruited to killing as an occupation?

WHO IS THE KILLER IN FELONY HOMICIDE CASES?

Before discussing killers, we need to decide which persons can be called killers in felony homicides. As has been stressed in this research, in most cases there is a group involved. All the members may be charged with murder and may actually be involved in stages of the killing. The police differentiate between the group members by labelling one or more of them as "shooters." The police are more concerned with convicting the "shooter" than the others. In cases where they believe the "shooter" is not the leader, but is acting under orders from another

---

Portions of this chapter were presented to the American Criminological Association Meetings, Dallas, 1978, under the title "Learning to Kill: Apprenticeships and On-the-Job Training."

member, they are also concerned with convicting the leader. It is difficult to decide if only the actual "shooter" should be considered a killer in these cases. In robbery groups, it is rarely only one member who does the killing. Many times the group members who will do the actual killing are the ones who own weapons.

The implication of this discussion is that in the eyes of the law all participants in a felony homicide are murderers. The police and courts believe, however, that the actual "shooter" (stabber, strangler, etc.) is the most culpable. They also recognize (the Manson case being a prime example), that the leader, the person who has the power over the actions of others, has greater responsibility. However, apart from the obvious leader and the "shooter," in any homicide the other members may support, encourage or discourage the killing. In some groups, members alternate assuming the killer role; in others the role is the property of one member.

Does it then require a unique person to be a killer? Is there a killer personality? The assumption has been made that violent behavior, including killing, is learned. But can anyone learn to kill? Not everyone, in even the most highly pro-violence subculture, will use violence; certainly not everyone will become a killer. Yokelson and Samenow (1976) have attempted to associate certain characteristics with the criminal personality. They describe this criminal personality as power-oriented and exploitive. They contend that the criminal must be able to fragment his thinking and depersonalize his victims. Certainly killers seem to be interested in themselves and lacking in concern for their victims. But this is also true of other criminals as well as people who are not criminals. Killers are distinguished from others only by their willingness to kill. Like other forms of deviance, killing may be a one-time aberration. That is, a person who kills once may not ever be willing to kill again. The person who goes on to have a career as a killer is one who evaluates killing in a positive way and who incorporates the killer role into his self-concept.

Although it is recognized that there are some real differences in robbery and contract killings, robbery killers and contract killers will be considered together as felony killers in the following discussion.

Ricardo, the contract killer who has been referred to throughout the book, considers robbery killers to be low class, no-style operators and contract killers to be the elite. By calling these killings impersonal, we do not mean that the killers and victims are not acquainted beforehand. In many cases they are. In fact, this is one of the problems that creates confusion in the statistics. These killings, where the victim and killer know each other, are more similar to stranger killings than to domestic or interpersonal conflict types. The fact that they are acquainted merely serves to make them potential victims, to make home entry possible or to put the victims off guard. The victims are not being selected due to personal animosity, but rather for "business reasons."

THE SELF-CONCEPT AND ROLE IDENTITIES

"The self in the symbolic interactionist perspective is a social object like all other social objects we share with others in interaction" (Charon, 1979:63). The self-concept of any person is composed of a number of role identities. They are the individual's imaginative view of him or herself being and acting in one role. Because the self is a social object who appraises, directs, criticizes and judges, that self must be identified and classified. Role identities refer to the names the self assumes and the self's social location relative to others. Role identities are social. While a person may aspire to confirm a particular identity, identities are supported, maintained, rejected and transformed via interaction with others. We make self-judgments based on our actions and our identities.

Role identities provide perspectives for appraising one's own thoughts and performances. It may be necessary for the actor to confirm his hypotheses by interacting with others (Horrocks and Jackson, 1972). Often, hypothesized identities are suggested tentatively to or by friends, and the actor considers their reactions. People who know the actor's personal style are able to envision how that person would perform in a given crime role and indicate just how suitable they think the role would be. While hypothesizing the role, the actor confirms how significant others feel about his or her crime status. Any role that is actually played in a crime may be fluid or enduring, may relate to isolated or multiple aspects of the self, and may become either a central or peripheral part of the self. In any case, the actor is likely to have considered and rehearsed the role.

THE KILLER ROLE IN SOCIETY

Social and professional roles are evaluated differently by various groups in society. Therefore, different segments of society may or may not approve of the male who aspires to the role of ballet dancer or car mechanic. In most societies the person who assumes a killer role is rejected. The act of killing has become more and more negatively evaluated, restricted, and limited to designated occupational roles. In modern North American society, killer roles are reserved for soldiers, police officers and public executioners. The killing act is elaborately rationalized and ritualized. The element of choice is removed so that persons who kill in these statuses are not labelled "killers." In order to be considered a murderer or a killer in modern society, the act has to be considered unnecessary and selfish, as opposed to altruistically motivated. Thus, within the law, and in the lay person's mind, it is only those who commit felony homicides who are labelled "killer." To most of society, it is a despised role.

THE KILLER ROLE IDENTITY IN CRIMINAL SUBCULTURES

The majority of persons who engage in felony homicides are career criminals. Much has been written about the way in which career criminals are able to rationalize their act to maintain their own self-esteem. As we have pointed out, different sets of norms and values are adopted by criminals (Irwin, 1970; Miller, 1978). Members of criminal groups must justify their killings to each other.

THE INCIDENTAL KILLER ROLE IDENTITY

The incidental killer is usually the individual in a robbery or sex crime who has not fully considered the implications of killing. This does not mean the person has not considered killing in general but rather that he has not specifically decided to do it in a particular situation. The incidental killer is the one who is least likely to incorporate the killer role as an enduring part of his or her self-concept. This person's mental rehearsal of the crime has avoided dealing with the results of killing. He thinks of part of the crime, such as the rape or robbery, but has used Scarlett O'Hara's tactic when dealing with the possibility of killing: he will think about it later. This means that he has not only avoided a decision on whether to kill, but has already provided a rationale for not having to consider himself as a killer. When at the scene and confronted with action that makes it necessary to kill, this person is able to use a justification of "self-defense." The following are examples of such rationalization. One is a group member charged with a murder who was not the shooter. The other is the shooter.

> We got in the store and one of the boys hollered "he got a pistol, he got a pistol" and then I heard about two or three shots, and then I saw a man, and then I hollered out, "You didn't have to shoot him, you didn't have to shoot him" and then I got scared. I snatched the money and ran out the door and we jumped in the car and drove off. When we got in the car I started crying; I said, "a man got shot." Everybody laughed at me. They called me a fool because I was crying. They said, "If you can't do it, you shouldn't be out here, you know." They thought I was stupid.

In the mental rehearsal of this robbery, the robber did not deal with the killing. In spite of being charged with murder, he does not think of himself as a murderer, although he himself had a gun. The possibility of killing had not been discussed by the members beforehand. Often the only discussion involves someone saying, "Do you want to do a rip?" then discussing weapons, location and entry tasks, but not the use of the guns for killing.

David, who has provided interview data on robbery homicides, is 21. He looks like a college student. He was involved in 6 murders, and over 200 robberies and rapes, before he was seventeen. In only one case was he the "shooter."

*The one where I did the shooting, well, after I felt
bad about that. I still don't know today if Donald
knew him or what, 'cause I told you he likes to
manipulate people. (Donald is the leader of the
group involved in the murder/robbery/rape crimes).
We were driving around the neighborhood looking
for a place and he keep coming back to this. Then
he says "go." This car pulls up. Donald says, "This
is it." Me and Dwayne got out and I grabbed this
girl and pulled her to the side so they couldn't see
us an' I told her to ring the bell and she did and
this boy come to the door and somehow managed to
pull her to the side. I couldn't see her and, I don't
know, maybe Dwayne pushed and he pulled and he
reached to the side of the door. I shot and Dwayne
shot and we run. I felt bad about that, not then but
after, like his family was from around the neighborhood and I passed the church a couple days later
and they were having the funeral. I felt bad about
that and thought I didn't need to shoot him, there
wasn't any reason. I could have ran.*

Although in both cases these men had been involved in
other crimes beforehand and had guns with them this
time, they didn't think of themselves as killers. David
had even been involved in crimes where people had
been killed, but he didn't think of these killings as relating to himself. In fact, if he thought about it at all he
merely thought about a murder rap as being "heavy"
time. Even though I presented him with several reasons
why he might have considered it justifiable to shoot, i.e.,
thinking it was a dope pad, thinking the victim had a
gun by the door, he said, "No, I didn't need to shoot the
guy." So David, although he may have used a "self-

defense justification" at the time, did not use it afterward. David does not conceive of himself as a killer. He thinks of himself as a criminal, a robber (thief) and rapist, but not a killer. And both men reported thinking of the killings as mistakes. The incidental killer is influenced by a particular situation. Even if not caught, as in the case of David, he may never take the shooter role again. The initial situation results in a re-evaluation of killing. The killer may have hypothesized this role before the actual encounter. He may have developed ideas about how he would act and feel during the crime which now need to be revised. If he does begin to think of himself as a killer, he will probably adopt one of the two roles that follow.

THE HOT KILLER ROLE IDENTITY

The hot killer prepares for murder by making himself enraged beforehand by getting into a state of being angry at the victim. Even when he has not made the decision to kill beforehand, awaiting the situation he will actually find on the scene, he has psyched himself up so that any little thing will be used as justification for getting angry enough to kill. Every action by a victim becomes personalized. Often the criminal will explain by saying that the victim "had an attitude," that is, that the victim did not show the proper respect and fear. But even when the victim does show respect and fear, there is always something that will allow the killer to become angry.

However, this process can be shut off at any time. Thus, if the situation changes, the rage is quickly turned off. Such killers are often feared by their colleagues. They see this rage as potentially being turned toward themselves, but they are able to differentiate this psuedo-expressive rage from real unpredictability by characterizing the person as "mean" as opposed to "crazy."

THE COOL KILLER ROLE IDENTITY

The cool killer, rather than personalizing an impersonal situation as the hot killer does, further depersonalizes it. The cool killer regards the killing as a task to be accomplished and concentrates on handling the details with efficiency. He often refers to the killing as work in which he takes pride. As Joey (Fisher, 1978: 54-5) says: "I've dabbled in just about every area of crime, but my specialty, the thing I do best, is kill people." He says further, "This is my job. It is my business. I shoot people and that's it." Where the incidental killer may panic and the hot killer may show rage, the cool killer copes with all situations without emotion. This lack of emotion often causes "cool killers" to be labelled psychopaths. My feeling is that it reflects a response style or way of handling situations of fear or danger and does not indicate inability to show emotion. Rather, it points up the ability to control emotional response. Both Henry and Ricardo, described in the following section, are examples of cool killers.

LEARNING TO KILL

We can begin to see that learning to kill does not occur entirely with the act of killing. It begins with thinking about killing and hypothesizing a killer identity for oneself and by defining the self as one who is ready to kill. Here there is a dichotomy. It is one thing to set limitations and consider oneself only able to kill in self defense or within a limited framework. Such killings are seen in the police or the army, where there is social approval of the act. Where the conception of being able to kill for profit exists, there is limited approval even among criminals. Perhaps this is the difference between the draftee and the mercenary in the army system.

Felony homicide is for the most part associated with a criminal career. In some cases the killer is an armed robber, arsonist, burglar, rapist or drug dealer. The killing is only involved in situations where the killer can assume another criminal identity. Some unspecialized career criminals may include killing as a part of their general careers. Only a few of the persons who commit felony homicides go on to careers as professional killers.

The following sections will deal with the actual process of learning how to kill.

PROGRESS IN VIOLENCE

As a person becomes involved in progressively more violent crimes leading to homicide, he gradually learns many of the techniques and skills needed for killing. The person has probably spent time in jail, so that the progression to homicide comes, as in the case of Henry, with shedding an unwillingness to kill.

> Henry was first approached about doing some killing when he was serving time with the man whom he eventually worked for. He was asked several times if he was hesitant about killing anyone. He told the man he was somewhat hesitant because he didn't want anyone to hurt his family. He talked it over with his wife and she convinced him that that kind of work wasn't for him. Later he made an agreement with the man that if there was any

money to be made he would be eligible for it. When he got out of prison he was approached by the man who said he had a person who needed to be killed and did he want the job. Henry says, "After I was approached, I talked it over with my relatives, with my wife. She was hesitant, you know, like she felt I shouldn't do that. But the money was kind of short. She was the only one working. Like I didn't have a job and it looked pretty skinny for me to get one, you know, so I accepted the offer."

Henry had many personal qualifications that influenced his recruitment. He was cool, unafraid and efficient. When the idea was presented to him originally, however, he thought it over and then turned it down. Yet he had already taken the beginning steps of thinking about it at the time and was sure he would have no problem in killing. Perhaps he partly accepted the evaluation and expectations of the men who approached him. When he did decide to accept the contract, he could transfer violence skills he already had to the killing situation. He also took time to consider several methods and had many consultations about how his first murder was going to be done. Henry then went into business as a killer. He talked things over with his family and went about his "work" methodically, eventually killing five people on two different occasions and wounding two others.

APPRENTICESHIP

Although the idea of apprenticeship in crime has been with us for a long time in criminology, it has not been explored to any extent in relation to homicide. There are two cases that I would like to describe that illustrate the murder apprenticeship. The first is Henry's son, Junior, who began his training by accompanying his father and mother on a multiple homicide when he was 17. Junior's mother had volunteered to act as driver as she was the only one with a valid driver's license.

> Junior's father instructed him in how to act when they got inside the store where the homicides were to take place. They simply waited around in the store until his father signaled the beginning by grabbing one of the girls who were to be killed. He sent the mother outside first so that she would not be in the store during the killings but the boy was allowed to remain. In this case he was simply to help and not to participate in the homicides. When he grabbed the second girl he sent Henry Jr. up to the front of the store to work the cash register. Then, after five minutes or so he came to the front of the store. He told Junior to get all the money from the register. Then he put him to work taking things from the store. He then instructed him to get cigarettes. He was loading things in the store and told Junior to get what he wanted. He had locked the intended victims in the bathroom. Then he told Junior to wait in the car.

Prior to entering the store, he gave Junior instructions on how to act. After they came out, he explained certain facets of the operation. He now knew that Junior would remain cool and was ready to advance to the next stage of killing—contact with and restraint of the victims.

Ricardo is 25. He is tall, attractive and articulate. He began his career as a drug dealer when he was about 15 and soon had 20 people working for him. He has served three years on a manslaughter charge, although by his own admission he was committing several murders a

month before he was caught and tried on one manslaughter conviction. Ricardo was talking about the legal
system and how easy it is to get away with murder.

Ricardo talks about his training.

> *I learned the majority of it—law—from my part-
> ners. They were older than me and they told me
> everything I needed to know about the police, what
> the police had to have for first degree murder, for
> second degree manslaughter. They knew a lot about
> the law. They used the law for their operations,
> what was best for them. So, all they did was told
> me how to go about doing it properly so they
> wouldn't have no evidence so I wouldn't get caught.
> As young as I was (about 16 or 17 at the time) and
> with sellin' drugs like I was, I took an' went on a
> couple things with them. We took quite a few jobs,
> you know, like goin' and collecting money for
> people, gettin' after a couple people, and after they
> dug the nerve that I had, like I wasn't goin' to let
> anyone take away my merchandise or dominate me
> in any way. They took an' offered me a couple jobs.
> I had been known to shoot already. Like the way it
> was I knew that for all the people I took out I'd
> have a lot of people in my corner. I knew if any-
> thing was to come down, they'd take care of it. I
> didn't have no record so the case would be dis-
> missed or I'd be charged with manslaughter and go
> to the penitentiary for two or three years.*

Ricardo's partners explained not only legal matters to
him, but details—how to get into a house, where to
catch intended victims, what to do at all times. They
told him, for example, not to listen to victims. If you did,
they would change your mind. They took him along just

to watch a few times. Finally, they gave him a contract for his first hit. He talks about his first hit and how he felt.

I was scared to death that first time I killed somebody because the guy grabbed me, you know, and I couldn't get loose of him. You know he had me like this here and I had a hard time getting his hands off my jacket, all his head blowed away, you know, it scared me. That was the first time, but after I went home and snorted some cocaine and heroin and drank me a fifth of liquor and smoked a ton of weed then I was kinda cool. Yeah, I was alright then. The first few times I kinda got this feeling in my stomach 'cause it be messy, you know. One guy I shot, I had his brains all over the side of my face and neck and clothes. But that's only when it's close like that—it's the only time I feel anything. I didn't have no problem because basically it involves trust and everyone likes me. I was liked by everybody and I was given better deals because of my relationships. And, I let the people know that I was dependable. So, soon I was taking out two or three people every couple weeks. When I did a job like I'd go out to the guy's house and we'd sit down and be talking about how we gonna do this or that or maybe we could get together on a project or take a trip somewhere. And, I'd look around to see if there were other people around and if there were then I'd make plans to meet him in some other part of town or come back and hit him later. But as soon as I drew my pistol I shot him because they'd try to get their own pistol or talk me out of it if I waited. Lot of guys, they start cryin', sweat pop out on their

head, they say "please don't kill me, I'll give you
$30,000, $40,000, anything you want" but I'm
gonna kill them because I got everything they got
anyhow.

Ricardo learned well. He has killed many times and
thinks of himself as a professional killer. He believes
that now he knows enough to continue committing per-
fect murders and not get caught. The only reason he'd
like to get out of the business is because he feels eventually "he'll end up in a trunk too." He says getting caught
saved his life.

Like I was getting careless. I was getting kind of hot.
Like I got so I thought I was so good like I'd take
and walk into Hudson's or in Recorder's Court and
shoot somebody.

RULES FOR PROFESSIONAL KILLERS

Ricardo has a number of rules that he observes when
killing that I have abstracted from his discussion. Here
are Ricardo's rules:
1. As soon as you accept the contract, act as quickly as
   possible so the victim won't suspect anything.
2. Be friendly and pleasant to your potential victims so
   they will like you. Killing them will be easier.
3. Don't talk about your crime to people; that's how
   most killers get caught.
4. Pick your own time and place; if it's not good, wait
   until later.
5. Keep the victim calm and relaxed as long as possible
   (this is also one of Henry's rules).
6. Don't let anyone place you near the crime scene.
7. Don't leave shell casings; they have fingerprints and
   help in tracing the gun.

8. After you draw your pistol, fire quickly.
9. Don't listen to the victim; you may hesitate.
10. Don't get too close to the victim; you may get grabbed or splattered.
11. Women, especially those in the dope business, should be killed too. Try to avoid killing when children are around.

Joey's rules are very similar to Ricardo's. He also speaks of isolating the victim, picking the proper place, acting quickly, not getting too close, not engaging in conversation, not involving other people, and disposing of the weapon (Fisher, 1973).

ON-THE-JOB TRAINING

While the apprenticeship in killing provides instructions and supervision, many killers learn to kill through on-the-job training. They begin by carrying guns and by engaging in criminal activity. For the most part they think about killing and want to do it. Often the criminal who kills on the spot does not intend to be a professional killer. This is a step that will move him into a more select rank of criminals and establish his reputation. The killer who learns on the job does not have the advantage of having the know-how that someone like Ricardo does. He has to rely on what he has heard and observed. He often wants to make sure that people know about the killing.

David, who was discussed earlier, belonged to a group of five to seven people who were involved in a large number of robberies, rapes and murders. Donald was the leader of this group. David said the first time any of them discussed murder was when Donald ran up to him on the street one day and said, "Hey, man, I just offed that guy that ripped off my brother's store. He's layin' there in the alley. You want to go and see?" David said, "You're crazy, man."

On another occasion Donald, David, and another member of the group had to go back to a house where Donald had shot someone. They were searching for cartridge cases that might have been left on the scene because Donald forgot to pick them up. In another murder the group was involved in, Donald, Dwayne and several others kidnapped two dope dealers whom they intended to hold for ransom. Donald called David and told him to come over. David describes the situation.

> *Donald took me into the corner to explain what was going on. They had these two guys tied up with tape on their mouths. Donald said he wanted me to call this guy's brother because Dwayne and Albert had already tried to call and had messed it up. I started to make the call but the operator cut in so I hung up. Then, me and Donald went to a phone booth and Donald called himself. Donald came back and started talking to the guy. The guy said, "Well, I told you not to call my brother. I told you my brother would call the police." The guy was like "don't bother me, man, you're the one that messed up." Then he started to torture the guy; he set his hair on fire. Then Donald told the guy, "I'm gonna kill you" and the guy said, "Do what you gotta do, man." The guy was cool and I respected him. He acted like a man and I wished we didn't have to kill him but I didn't say anything because I didn't know what they'd do. I knew there'd be trouble with Donald and I was afraid he'd think I was soft or something and then I knew Donald would come after me.*

Me and Donald took the other guy in the car. I was driving and then Donald leaned over and tried to strangle him but he was kicking too much. So we stopped and went in the alley and Donald took him out and shot him.

Although Donald was the leader and did much of the killing in this group, at least three of the other group members had killed on separate occasions and had assisted in others. In several cases, they had great difficulty in accomplishing the killing because they thought they would be able to use techniques like strangling or bludgeoning and the victims proved to be difficult to kill in that manner. They had to learn as they went along. They made many mistakes, although they still managed to escape being caught for a long time. They definitely did not operate efficiently as did the apprenticeship group. The following is another illustration of a robbery/homicide group who committed eleven homicides, five of which were multiple murders. In this case the murders were committed after the killers had been in the house for about an hour. After twenty minutes of conversation with the female victim, they tied her up in the bedroom. When the male victim came in, they also tied him. Willie describes the killing.

Gerald grabbed two portable TVs and took them downstairs to the car. When he came back upstairs he cut the cord off the iron and started to choke the guy with the cord. While he was doing that I went to the kitchen and got a knife out of the drawer and went to the bedroom where the girl was and struck her two or three times in the neck. I think it was on the left side. Then I took the knife out of her neck and wiped it off. I walked down the hall to the other bedroom where Gerald was still choking the guy. Gerald took the knife and stabbed the guy in the neck too. Then we went downstairs to the car. We took all the stuff to Gerald's house and we all fell asleep.

In this case it is obvious that they tried two different methods and then learned that one worked better than the other. In each of these cases the killers learned how to kill on the spot. They often used methods that were not effective and had to try other ways. Once they learned that they were able to kill and that they didn't mind killing, the killer role was incorporated into their self-concepts. None of the members of these groups came to regard their role as their primary identities, as did the individuals in the apprenticeship and progress-in-violence categories. There are some criminals, however, who learn through experience, become proficient, and then change identities. They move from criminals who occasionally kill to killers who may slowly abandon other types of crime.

The preceding discussion attempted to consider how a killer role identity develops. Several killer role identities were examined as well as the processes of learning to kill.

THE PROFESSIONAL KILLER

Regardless of the means by which a person comes to learn how to kill, not every killer goes on to think of himself[1] as a pro—an iceman or hitman. Like other professional criminals, the professional killer thinks of himself as a specialist, having unique skills and training and taking pride in the way he conducts himself in his work.

---

1. So far as I can tell, although women participate in felony murders, none are described as professionals.

The rationalizations regarding killing give way to the acceptance of the self as a person who does killing for a living or at least to supplement his income. If there are not justifications for any given killing, however, the professional killer must develop some. He needs to rid himself of his inner doubts and also doubts about the way in which other people may regard him. While the exact nature of criminal activities may be concealed from family and friends, working associates are aware of the professional killer's role identity.

The professional killer is not feared by others because he is seen as killing only under orders or in a contract situation. Associates are only fearful if they have violated rules or are perceived as targets because of their own criminal activities. The professional killer recognizes that he is killing purely for profit. Ricardo said, "I suppose there must be something left out of me because you are supposed to feel something and I don't feel anything." Henry also did not appear to have any feeling for his victims, nor did David. It was not sympathy for the victims that kept David from going on to become a professional like Henry and Ricardo. He simply didn't see killing as his type of work. The hit man, like the robber, sees his work as requiring nerve. He tends to see killing as wielding the ultimate power. All of the hit men seem to respect their own killing abilities as something that sets them apart, makes them unique and somehow better than others. The glorification of their work seems an adequate rationalization for the professionals.

Essentially then, many killers develop role identities as killers but only for a few does this role identity continue to the extent that they think of themselves as professionals. They learn to kill and develop their skills in several ways. Their own responses to their initial killings, as well as those of others significant to them are influential in their evaluations of themselves in the killer role and influence whether or not they will continue to kill. Those who kill incidentally and who define their actions as defensive are less likely to accept the idea of killing for profit and accept themselves as killers.

9 Some Final Thoughts

In this study, felony homicide has been described as group-based socially-learned conduct. Chapter 9 will review some of the major themes that have been discussed and raise questions for future research.

THE MEANING OF FELONY HOMICIDE

The reader has been invited to view felony homicide for what it is—a cruel, inhumane, and predatory form of behavior. It is frightening to realize that this type of homicide is increasing. Killing for profit is different from killing for personal reasons, because the victim in a felony homicide is disregarded and is considered insignificant. Thus the intent in felony homicide is criminal. Yet, as has been shown, felony homicide is a rational act committed by people who are aware of what they are doing.

SOCIAL AND ENVIRONMENTAL SUPPORTS AND CONSTRAINTS

The use of violence for achieving various goals receives support in certain segments of society. It is particularly true in criminal subcultures that violence is recognized as an accepted means of controlling and punishing others who violate group rules. It is also a means to achieve goals of money and success. Even those who kill professionally are aware, however, that violence cannot be used indiscriminately or they will end up in trouble themselves.

In a sense, the community in which killers interact has the characteristics of a closed society. Killers rarely interact with persons outside of their community other than occasional family members and victims. When they are confronted with the disgust or disapproval of law-abiding members of society, they must face what they do and are and how the non-criminal world sees them. Ricardo mentioned that some of his noncriminal friends from high school and family members disapproved and shunned him. He rationalized his feelings of rejection saying, "I felt bad at first but who needs those people? I make more money in a week than they do in six months. Besides, I'd rather hang around with my own friends anyhow." For the most part, criminals keep their associations in the criminal world where they are accepted and tolerated, if not approved. As they have increasingly limited their contacts with people outside this subculture, they tend to view the outside world as very similar to their own. David said of the police officers he dealt with, "You know, they're no different from me. They lookin' out for themselves, got their nice ride and clothes. A few of them really care about us but most of them, they don't care. They just take care of business. Only difference is they on the right side of the law."

THE IMPORTANCE OF THE GROUP

In this study it has been stressed repeatedly that felony homicide is a group-based activity. Most criminal groups tolerate killing as a means of punishment within their own groups. They accept certain criminal activities even if they are not part of these activities themselves. The groups that become involved in felony homicides usually accept the idea of killing for gain. They tolerate and often encourage killing by members of their group even if they are not involved themselves. In many of the groups discussed in this study, the willingness to kill or to go along with killing is taken for granted by the group members when criminal activities are planned or executed. Group tolerance of rape, robbery, torture and killing has been demonstrated repeatedly, and there have been indications that this conduct can be limited or controlled if the group expects it to be. Further, it has been shown that felony murders are oversimplified when viewed as dyadic interactions, as they frequently involve conflicting groups and are performed before audiences of peripherally involved and uninvolved witnesses. Group observation and evaluation of killing performances are influential on both the killers and the victims. Their influence on these killer performances should not be minimized.

VARIATIONS IN TYPES OF FELONY HOMICIDE

Only three types of felony homicide have been elaborated in this study. These constitute the most common types—robbery homicides, executions, and sexual assaults. It has been stressed that the motive in all of these cases is profit usually by means of taking possessions by force. Profit can be creditability, money and goods, lives or sexual favors. The general intent in these cases is criminal, but distinctions have been made as to whether the specific or primary intent was robbery, killing or sex. Other distinctions have been made regarding the tasks and types of groups involved. Similarities were also pointed out with regard to objectification and lack of concern both for the victim and within the criminal group.

STAGES IN FELONY HOMICIDES

The sequential acts in felony homicides were described. It was shown that this type of homicide is preceded by a criminal planning stage, however short. It then moves to a stage of interaction with the victim, and finally a post-homicide stage. It is important in understanding the planning and organization of these killings to observe the negotiations, situation structuring, and defining that go on prior to the encounter. One must also look at the interactions that occur between the criminals involved during the encounter. It has been pointed out that a major difference between felony and social conflict homicides is the periods of interaction prior to and after the homicide when the victim is not present. The commitment to carry out the act, the testing of attitudes and the group's expectations that occur during these periods before and after the killing are very important to both the shooters and other group members in their handling of the planned homicide and subsequent homicides.

PATTERNS OF CONDUCT IN HOMICIDE INTERACTIONS

Another major section of the study focused on patterns of conduct between victims and killers, and between killer group members. Certain patterns are found repeatedly in these cases. These define the situations for the participants and move the action along. If these actions are viewed in the context of the situation, we may eventually be able to assess their influence on subsequent killer and victim acts. Defining and describing these common patterns seems to be a necessary first step.

KILLER ROLE IDENTITY, SELF-CONCEPT, AND CAREER CONTINGENCIES

One major question arising in this study is how the person who does the actual killing deals with his role vis-á-vis his self-concept. It was pointed out that a number of rationalizations permit killing and that these are related to the type of homicide and to the kind of killer role identity that develops. Several ways of becoming a killer or of learning the skills and tasks involved were examined. These ranged from specific training or apprenticeship types of learning, to on-the-job learning in which the killers incorporated generally learned information with trial and error actions.

WHO BECOMES INVOLVED IN FELONY HOMICIDES AND WHY?

The position taken in this book is that felony homicides are primarily committed by career criminals or at least by people who have accepted the norms and values of violence-approving criminal subcultures.

It has also been suggested that not every person who accepts the values and norms in this subculture will be willing or able to kill. What, then, decides which members of the subculture kill and which do not? First, opportunity. One must have the opportunity to kill and before that, the opportunity to consider killing seriously. Some criminals, as they become involved in crime activities, get involved in nonviolent criminal activities and find that they have talents in those directions. Others have their initial experiences with robbery or rape and find these activities to their liking. What else decides who will kill? A second consideration is group influence. The particular crime group that the killer

joins is very influential in developing his or her acceptance of killing. A third factor is whether the individual
is able to envision himself as a killer. If a criminal
conceives of himself as a killer it may have been suggested by someone who saw the person as fit for the
role. The criminal may, at that time, reject the role as
unacceptable just as many people could not envision
themselves as artists or doctors. Those who are able to
imagine themselves in the role may then seek out or
have thrust upon them a chance to test the role, evaluate
their performance, and decide whether or not to continue. In their own comments, career killers like "Joey"
(Fisher, 1975) and Ricardo preface their advance into
their career as a killer by saying: "I learned that I could
kill" or "I found out I was able to kill." This knowledge
changes them, whether or not they go on to become
professional killers. They think of themselves as being
able to kill. In some descriptions, being able to kill is
seen as the ultimate masculine act and is associated with
control, nerve, and courage. Throughout the literature
on personal violent confrontations, there are references
to "having the balls" to risk injury or one's life.

MOTIVES AND JUSTIFICATIONS

Motivation in interpersonal homicides tend to be ego
related. The intention is to control, punish, or resolve a
conflict with an uncooperative victim whose personal
involvement with the killer is an essential characteristic
of the killing. The motivation in felony homicides is
primarily acquisitive; that is, the killer wishes to acquire
or maintain sex, goods, money or a business reputation.
He can avoid socially expected costs in work, social
relationship with the the victim or contact with legitimate authorities. The gain is thus personal profit and

avoids interpersonal conflict. Several tactics are used to rationalize the act; depersonalizing victims or personalizing their acts, defensively interpreting situations as doing a public service, denigrating the victim, and glorifying the killer role.

Persons who engage in felony homicide do so for the same reasons that they engage in other criminal activities. Many are able to gain material things they could not have through legitimate means. Beyond that, there is an excitement and sense of power that many find attractive. In addition, they enjoy the fear and respect of their peers.

AREAS FOR FURTHER RESEARCH

Research that focuses on felony homicide is just beginning to develop. There are a number of areas that have not been touched in the research or that need further expansion.

THE ROLE OF THE WEAPON IN FELONY HOMICIDE

The role of the weapon in homicides which is examined statistically by Fisher (1976) and Zimring (1972, 1977) needs further work of the sort done by Conklin (1972). Conklin has looked at the functions of the weapon in robbery. More needs to be done on the meaning of weapons to killers and other participants in homicides. The fact that so many people are armed and ready to use weapons suggests consensual meanings for some killers and victims. What do arms mean to those victims having no contacts with weapons or criminal subcultures?

THE AWARENESS OF SENTENCE LENGTH IN RELATIONSHIP TO THE DECISION TO KILL

Many studies have examined the relationship of the death penalty to homicide rates (Sellin, 1967; Jaywardene, 1977). However, more research is needed on the expectations of long sentences in felony cases and how they influence the decision to kill. In the interview with Ricardo and David, both mentioned their awareness of the types of sentences for murder and spoke of their thoughts on punishment. It becomes obvious from their conversations that they are not too concerned with serving long prison sentences. Their expectations of being able to "get away with murder" develop from their experiences as criminals and from interaction with other criminals. Their knowledge of criminal justice procedures and rules of evidence and of plea bargaining allow them to consider engaging in a variety of crimes, including murder. They assess the risk of long sentences as minimal. When a group is awaiting trial on felony homicide cases, it becomes a real challenge for the police. They must prevent members from turning around evidence. It is their job to see that witnesses not receive messages that threaten, coax, or bribe them not to testify. The criminals' messages to each other indicate their awareness of prosecution's difficulties in getting a conviction for these cases. Skogan (1978) refers to a study in which burglars avoid confrontations with victims, fearing the heavy sentences associated with violent crimes. So some evidence does exist to show that certain criminals are deterred by fear of heavy sentences, while others are not.

THE ROLE OF WOMEN IN FELONY HOMICIDES

Although there has been some research on female murderers (Cole, 1968), it has focused primarily on interpersonal conflict killings or the occasional one exception. The Detroit data suggest that there is more involvement of women in these cases than might be expected. Although it has been traditional for women to play minor roles as career criminals, there appears to be more role equality in robbery and execution killings than appeared on the surface. Although women were often used to gain entrance or to help set up a social visit scene in robberies and executions, they also were involved in planning, controlling and guarding victims, robbing, torturing and occasionally in the actual killing. As victims, women seemed to move from traditional and secondary roles to roles of primary targets. They were involved in the criminal activities and had access to and used weapons. Although women are only a small proportion of the perpetrators in these cases, there does appear to be more equality in their roles than was expected. Their involvement needs further investigation.

EXPECTATION STATES AND AWARENESS CONTEXTS

The concept of awareness contexts (Glaser and Strauss, 1964) was raised in reference to the question of whether the victims knew if the perpetrator had a killer role identity and the extent to which the victims maintained or acted on this knowledge. Another area that needs further exploration is the evaluation of external status characteristics. Killers and victims must be observed as they develop performance expectations for each other in these encounters. Does the involvement in a situation such as a rape, robbery, or execution result in the branding of identities such as rapist, robber, or killer for all of the participants? Can a killer identity and the expectation of the victim be responsible for what appears to be incautious or foolhardy behavior on the part of victims? Or is the foolhardy conduct more likely if a different motive is attributed? More intensive research with intended victims and witnesses is necessary to determine how they make their decisions to engage in behavior such as resistance, escape, or begging. How united or separate do they perceive group members as being and on what basis? The role-taking process that occurs in these encounters for both victims and killers significantly affects the performances of both. Hence the processes and characteristics which label each group are compounded by the danger and emotionality of the particular situation.

ROLE IDENTITY AND COMPARTMENTALIZATION

As we mentioned earlier, some people do not accept the killer role identity. Even after they have enacted the role, they rationalize their motives (e.g., taking money by killing vs. making money). They see the act as transient and situational. Even after murdering, some of the killers continue to think of themselves as dope men or robbers. The others appear to compartmentalize the role as an occupation. Is it possible to have the identity of a professional killer, and still maintain a separate identity? In discussing this with Ricardo, who identified himself as a professional (actually, he used the term semiprofessional) killer, he was asked if the role made people afraid of him. He said that some people he knew were afraid and would no longer associate with him. He found this difficult to understand. It appears then that for him this identity was strictly occupational. He could not see what his occupation had to do with the way he related to people personally. Essentially, this is the same cognitive process as that used by the police officer and soldier. However, with police and soldiers, killing is only a part of their activities. With the "professional

killer," the killing is the main activity. Further research
is needed to determine how killing is used in interpersonal conflicts by robbery and sex killers and by contract
killers.

FEAR AND EXCITEMENT IN FELONY HOMICIDE

David, when speaking of performing his crimes, mentioned that he was scared throughout the crime until it
was finished. Also, he found performing the crimes
addicting. Einstadter (1974) has examined the stressful
and exciting nature of robbery and the element of con-
quering risk. He compared it with dangerous sport activities. How do this stress, fear, and excitement influence the homicide aspect of robberies? Is it the same
for executions? It seems likely that defining the situational risk is likely to increase the group's chances of
making the decision to kill. It also gives the criminals
more opportunity to define the situation defensively.
The robber or rapist may decide to kill if the victim
screams or resists. The possibility that killing might be
involved may add to the fear and excitement. Does this
mean then that in executions, where the decision to kill
has been finalized, the unknown thrill aspect is reduced? Is the danger sufficient to produce these feelings or does a prior commitment to kill have an effect
on the stress-producing nature of the interaction? Contract killers do not appear to initiate or seek out encounters, as do robbery and sex killers. Perhaps the fear
and excitement or the "addiction" is missing, or perhaps killing as a primary motive creates more lasting
feelings. A more thorough investigation is needed to
see if these feelings occur in executions and if there are
different feelings occurring in robbery and sex homicides from those in executions.

THE DIFFUSION OF RESPONSIBILITY

One final area that has emerged from viewing group felony homicides is the need for a more careful analysis of the impact of the group in taking responsibility for the killing. As we know, in law, the criminal justice system holds all members of the felony homicide group responsible. In practice, leaders and shooters are considered most culpable. Among the group members themselves, however, the number of criminals provides a lessening of the responsibility for the act. First, it divides the killers into "we" and "they," which is less personal than "me" and "you." Second, the group, rather than the individual, agrees on the crime. Third, the killing can be defined as an act to support or defend another member. This is considered "nobler" than self-defense. It brings the other members closer together. Fourth, there is the question of the "risky shift" (Shaw, 1976), the idea that a group will make decisions that are more daring or dangerous than the individual would make. Hence, if the group participating does not make overt protests against killing, the individual can assume it is the group's decision rather than his own. More systematic research must be done to follow up some of David's ideas. Would Dwayne do anything Donald wanted him to? Would David himself not voice a protest over killing because he didn't want the group's disapproval? The main question is how many of these killings are based on group encouragement, approval and support (Milgrim, 1964). Are some of them, such as sex homicides, done to avoid group disapproval?

THE INFLUENCE OF GROUP LEADERS

It has been found that there is relative equality among members of robbery groups (Einstadter, 1966). This is true to some extent in homicide groups as well; however, there seem to be leaders in many of these groups. Much leadership is functional and distributed, but some is more charismatic. Further research should compare egalitarian or distributed leadership groups with those that have visible leaders. Are there differences in the continuation of the killing pattern with the leader's influence? Is killing more likely when equal status group members support the act?

SUMMARY

In summary, the findings of this study are:
1. Felony homicide is a discrete form of murder characterized by impersonality, instrumentality, and profit motivation.
2. Felony homicides frequently involve more than the shooter-victim dyad, often having victim and killer groups and a witness audience.
3. The three major sub-types of felony homicide presented, robbery homicide, executions, and sex killings, are similar with respect to impersonality, instrumentality and general motivation. They differ in specific intent, justifications, tasks and, to some extent, group involvement.
4. There are some consistent interaction patterns between killers and victims and within homicide groups.
5. The killer role identity is hypothesized, tested, and incorporated or rejected as part of the actor's self concept.
6. Professional and career killers centralize the role identity. It becomes an important aspect of their identification by self and by others.

Appendix
Statistical Data, Detroit Police
Department Homicide Unit

TABLE A.1
TYPES OF HOMICIDES, 1926–80

Year	Murder & Man-slaughter	Cleared	Not Cleared	Excus-able	Justifiables: Police	Citizen	Man-slaughter by Neg-ligence	Total	Percent Cleared Total
1926	225	133	92	56	45	—	—	326	72%
1927	131	95	36	59	42	—	—	232	84%
1928	120	94	26	59	27	—	—	206	87%
1929	158	111	47	49	38	—	—	245	81%
1930	114	87	27	47	31	—	—	192	86%
1931	107	91	16	37	16	—	—	160	90%
1932	96	76	20	32	21	—	—	149	87%
1933	78	65	13	26	15	—	—	119	89%
1934	60	52	8	20	10	—	—	90	91%
1935	60	55	5	23	7	—	—	90	94%
1936	66	60	6	23	14	—	—	103	94%
1937	74	56	18	22	13	—	—	109	83%
1938	55	49	6	15	13	—	—	83	93%
1939	60	51	9	23	6	—	—	89	89%
1940	66	59	7	14	14	1	—	95	93%
1941	57	53	4	21	7	1	2	88	95%
1942	48	42	6	41	5	—	—	94	94%
1943	79	65	14	18	28	—	—	125	88%
1944	73	64	9	29	8	2	—	112	92%

(continued on next page)

Table A.1 continued

Year	Murder & Man-slaughter	Cleared	Not Cleared	Excus-able	Justifiables: Police	Justifiables: Citizen	Man-slaughter by Neg-ligence	Total	Percent Cleared Total
1945	71	59	12	30	11	2	—	114	89%
1946	85	78	7	24	8	—	—	117	94%
1947	86	73	13	26	7	2	—	121	89%
1948	89	85	4	16	7	—	5	117	97%
1949	91	86	5	12	10	4	—	117	96%
1950	97	85	12	16	4	1	—	118	90%
1951	105	96	9	24	7	—	—	136	93%
1952	86	80	6	23	2	—	—	111	95%
1953	103	92	11	27	2	—	1	133	92%
1954	95	88	7	13	5	3	2	118	94%
1955	121	109	12	19	4	2	—	146	92%
1956	89	76	13	16	4	2	—	111	88%
1957	103	94	9	16	6	1	—	126	92%
1958	91	83	8	19	2	2	2	116	93%
1959	98	91	7	8	6	2	13	127	94%
1960	119	109	10	31	4	2	1	157	94%
1961	108	101	7	28	2	2	1	141	95%
1962	113	101	12	24	3	—	3	143	92%
1963	103	93	10	23	5	3	3	137	93%
1964	104	94	10	21	6	5	2	138	93%

Year	Murder & Man-slaughter	Cleared	Not Cleared	Excus-able	Justifiables: Police	Citizen	Man-slaughter by Neg-ligence	Total	Percent Cleared Total
1965	148	132	16	40	9	4	3	204	91%
1966	175	148	27	39	7	10	1	232	88%
1967	220	189	31	61	33	14	4	332	90%
1968	303	244	59	86	13	18	3	423	86%
1969	354	260	94	84	13	31	6	488	81%
1970	413	282	131	81	20	30	6	550	80.5%
1971	508	289	219	89	43	54	16	690	70.1%
1972	528	305	223	73	36	42	14	693	72%
1973	616	328	288	56	29	34	16	751	67%
1974	653	421	232	61	30	29	18	801	75%
1975	555	367	188	52	29	40	9	685	77%
1976	622	415	207	42	23	26	10	723	73%
1977	427	295	132	51	18	14	18	528	75%
1978	451	*	*	47	18	11	15	542	80.2%
1979	407	*	*	44	16	17	9	493	78%
1980	487	*	*	61	13	16	6	583	74%

* Breakdown not available for these years.

203

TABLE A.2
PROFILE OF SELECTED FELONY HOMICIDE CASES
FROM 1972, 1973, 1975, 1976, 1977

Cases	Victims	Execu-tions	Robberies	Drugs	Multiple	Bound
655	781	612	158	86	54	133

TABLE A.3
TYPES OF FELONY CASES, 1974

Type	Number	Percent	Cumulative Percent
Attempted Robbery/ Robbery Homicide	119	39.7	39.7
Robbery Execution/ Execution Style	42	14.0	53.7
Executions, Contracts, Revenge	110	36.7	90.4
Sex	13	4.3	94.7
Mixed Motive with Sex and/or Robbery	9	3.0	97.7
Murder (unclassified)	7	2.3	100
Total	300 [a]	100	100

a. Cases with multiple victims were treated as one case.

TABLE A.4
TYPES OF NON-FELONY CASES, 1974

Type	Number [a]	Percent	Cumulative Percent
Social Conflict Close Relationship	94	23.1	23.1
Social Conflict	187	46.0	69.1
Attempted Robbery, Arson, Extortion	46	11.3	80.4
Police Shooting	12 [b]	3.0	83.4
Accident	20	5.0	88.4
Murder	27	6.6	95.0
Unknown	20	5.0	100.0
Total	406 [c]	100.0	100.0

a. Cases with multiple victims were treated as one case.
b. Twenty cases of police shootings were omitted from the sample due to lack of data.
c. Six cases were either missing from the files or ruled suicide.

TABLE A.5
AGE OF PERPETRATOR, 1974

| | FELONY | | | NON-FELONY | | |
Age	Number	Percent	Cumu-lative Percent	Number	Percent	Cumu-lative Percent
16 and under	9	4.8	4.8	18	4.8	4.8
17 to 20	60	32.1	36.9	38	10.0	14.8
21 to 25	59	31.6	68.5	82	21.7	36.5
26 to 30	34	18.2	86.7	68	18.0	54.5
31 to 35	15	8.0	94.7	50	13.3	67.8
36 to 40	7	3.7	98.4	29	7.7	75.5
41 to 45	1	0.5	98.9	23	6.1	81.6
46 to 50	2	1.1	100.0	23	6.1	87.7
51 to 55	0	0.0	—	16	4.2	91.9
56 to 60	0	0.0	—	10	2.7	94.6
61 to 65	0	0.0	—	8	2.1	96.7
Over 65	0	0.0	—	12	3.2	99.9 [a]
Total	187	100.0	100.0	377	99.9 [a]	99.9 [a]
Unknown	133			29		
	320			406		

a. Equals slightly less than 100 percent due to rounding.

TABLE A.6
AGE OF VICTIM, 1974

	FELONY			NON-FELONY		
Age	Number	Percent	Cumu-lative Percent	Number	Percent	Cumu-lative Percent
12 and under	3	1.0	1.0	11	2.7	2.7
13 to 20	33	11.0	12.0	57	14.1	16.8
21 to 25	71	23.9	35.9	91	22.6	39.4
26 to 30	42	14.1	50.0	65	16.1	55.5
31 to 35	28	9.3	59.3	53	13.2	68.7
36 to 40	17	5.7	65.0	31	7.7	76.4
41 to 45	17	5.7	70.7	29	7.2	83.6
46 to 50	17	5.7	76.4	24	6.0	89.6
51 to 55	20	6.7	83.1	21	5.2	94.8
56 to 60	16	5.3	88.4	9	2.2	97.0
61 to 65	7	2.4	90.8	4	1.9	98.9
65 and over	27	9.1	99.9 [b]	8	1.9	100.8 [c]
Total	298 [a]	99.9 [b]	99.9 [b]	403	100.8 [c]	100.8 [c]

a. Victim age unknown in 2 cases.
b. Equals less than 100 percent due to rounding.
c. Equals more than 100 percent due to rounding.

TABLE A.7
NUMBER OF PERPETRATORS PER CASE, 1974

Perpe-trator	FELONY			NON-FELONY		
	Number	Percent	Cumu-lative Percent	Number	Percent	Cumu-lative Percent
One	71	33.0	33.0	370	93.6	93.6
Two	64	29.7	62.7	16	4.1	97.7
Three	45	20.9	83.6	6	1.5	99.2
Four	25	11.6	95.2	1	.2	99.4
Five	9	4.3	99.5	1	.2	99.6
Over Five	1	.4	99.9	1	.2	99.8
Total	215	99.9 [a]	99.9 [a]	395	99.8 [a]	99.8 [a]
Unknown	85			11		
Total Cases	300			406		

a. Equals less than 100 percent due to rounding.

TABLE A.8

NUMBER OF VICTIMS PER CASE, 1974

Victims	FELONY			NON-FELONY		
	Number	Percent	Cumu- lative Percent	Number	Percent	Cumu- lative Percent
One	271	90.3	90.3	394	97.0	97.0
Two	24	8.0	98.3	11	2.7	99.7
Three	3	1.0	99.3	1	0.2	99.9 [a]
Four	2	0.7	100.0	0	0.0	99.9 [a]
Total	300	100.0	100.0	406	99.9 [a]	99.9 [a]

a. Equals less than 100 percent due to rounding.

TABLE A.9
SEX OF VICTIMS ONE AND TWO, 1974

	FELONY				NON-FELONY			
Sex	V1	Per-cent	V2	Per-cent	V1	Per-cent	V2	Per-cent
Male	248	82.7	16	53.3	340	83.9	9	75
Female	52	17.3	14	46.6	65	16.0	3	25
Total	300	100.0	30	100.0	405 [a]	100.0	12	100

a. Missing data: 1 case.

TABLE A.10
SEX OF KNOWN PERPETRATORS ONE AND TWO, 1974

	FELONY				NON-FELONY			
Sex	P1	Per-cent	P2	Per-cent	P1	Per-cent	P2	Per-cent
Male	207	96.7	118	84.9	306	77.5	21	87.5
Female	7	3.3	21	15.1	89	22.5	3	12.5
Total	214	100.0	139	100.0	395	100.0	24	100.0

TABLE A.11
TYPE OF WEAPON USED, 1974

Weapon	FELONY			NON-FELONY		
	Number	Percent	Cumu-lative Percent	Number	Percent	Cumu-lative Percent
Handgun	172	57.5	57.5	184	53.5	53.5
Rifle	19	6.3	63.8	30	8.7	62.2
Shotgun	15	5.0	68.8	43	12.5	74.7
Bludgeon	8	2.7	71.5	11	3.2	77.9
Combined	15	5.0	76.5	4	1.2	79.1
Knife	42	14.0	90.5	63	18.3	97.4
Personal Weapons	20	6.7	97.2	9	2.6	100.0
Drowning, Asphyxiation	7	2.3	99.5	—	—	—
Unknown	1	.3	.3	—	—	—
Totals	299[a]	99.8[b]	99.8[b]	344[a]	100.0	100.0

a. Missing data: 1 felony, 62 non-felony.
b. Equals less than 100 due to rounding.

TABLE A.12
VICTIM RESTRAINED (BOUND OR GAGGED), 1974

	FELONY			NON-FELONY		
	Number	Percent	Cumu-lative Percent	Number	Percent	Cumu-lative Percent
Unknown	4	1.3	1.3	6	1.5	1.5
No	244	82.2	83.5	399	98.2	99.7
Yes	49	16.5	100.0	1	.2	99.9
Totals	297[a]	100.0	100.0	406	99.9[b]	99.9[b]

a. Missing data: 3 cases.
b. Equals less than 100 percent due to rounding.

TABLE A.13
VICTIM RESISTED, 1974

	FELONY			NON-FELONY		
	Number	Percent	Cumu-lative Percent	Number	Percent	Cumu-lative Percent
Unknown	20	6.8	6.8	18	6.0	6.0
No	144	48.7	55.5	133	44.3	50.3
Yes	104	35.1	90.6	99	33.0	83.3
Had Weapon	26	9.4	100.0	50	16.7	100.0
Total	294[a]	100.0	100.0	300[b]	100.0	100.0

a. Missing data: 4 cases.
b. 106 data missing due to difficulty in assigning this condition in social conflict cases.

TABLE A.14

VICTIM TORTURED OR ASSAULTED, 1974

	FELONY			NON-FELONY		
	Number	Percent	Cumu-lative Percent	Number	Percent	Cumu-lative Percent
Unknown	3	1.0	1.0	6	2.0	2.0
None	218	73.4	74.4	236	80.0	82.0
Torture	32	10.8	85.2	5	1.7	83.7
Assault	40	13.5	98.7	47	15.9	99.6
Rape	4	1.2	99.9 [b]	1	.3	99.9 [b]
Total	297 [a]	3 99.9 [b]	99.9 [b]	295 [c]	99.9 [b]	99.9 [b]

a. Missing data: 3 cases.
b. Equals less than 100 percent due to rounding.
c. 111 missing data due to difficulty in designating victim assault in social conflict cases, often recorded simply as altercation.

Glossary
General Terms and Special Terms Related to Felony and Non-Felony Cases

after hours joint: place that sells liquor after the legal hours, often in a house or apartment.

B & E: Breaking and entering.

cap: kill.

cohab: term used in this research to designate any living-together relationship in which there is a sexual liaison.

contract: money offered or paid for a killing; an agreement to kill for a set price.

do: an amount of heroin to be used for a single injection, a fix, a hit.

dope men: the middle and upper level drug dealers who are recognized as influential in the drug community.

dudes: males, as in bad dude, cool dude.

end up in a trunk: become the victim of an execution, especially in Detroit, where leaving victims in car trunks was a relatively common practice in the '70s.

215

execution: a deliberate premeditated murder, a murder in which the victims are tied or blindfolded.

execution-style: a robbery or sex murder in which victims are restrained, blindfolded.

get a blow: to purchase or acquire heroin or cocaine or a mixture for snorting through the nose.

get an attitude: to show scorn, disapproval or superiority, verbally or nonverbally, so that it is visible to others.

get valiant: to come on to another in an aggressive, threatening manner.

goes down: takes place. A person might be referred to as "being there when the crime goes down."

half key: ½ of a kilo (2.2 lbs).

half spoon: a measure of heroin which varies from one drug group to another. In Detroit's black drug group this may refer to ½ plastic stirring spoon from McDonald's.

heavy time: a long prison sentence, a relatively long sentence for a particular type of crime.

hit: to kill.

hit man: professional or hired killer; also ice man.

hit on me: to make a sexual overture.

jive: heroin; also jones, stuff, shit.

lady: woman with whom there is established relationship; in place of girlfriend.

leg buster: hired muscle, person who uses force, derived from breaking of leg bones with baseball bat.

mark: person who is victim or potential victim of deception or criminal act. Also, john or trick.

mixed jive: street level heroin that has been cut with milk, sugar or other product.

off: to kill.

on the street: refers to information that is common knowledge throughout the community.

P: high quality heroin (*pure*); refers to heroin that has not been cut to street level, also known as *raw* heroin.

player: person who is recognized as part of criminal community; pimp.

P–38: A .38 caliber pistol, usually a Walther, a preferred weapon.

professional killer: a hired killer, one who kills for money.

putting out a paper: offering a contract on a victim; letting it be known that you will pay to have someone killed.

ride: car.

rip off: robbery.

self-serving statement: an account of a crime in which the teller minimizes his or her involvement and culpability.

shooter: person in a felony homicide who actually does the killing.

up front: before the act takes place; for example, paying for a killing before it is accomplished.

TERMS RELATED TO FELONY CASES

attempted robbery murder: cases in which robbery is attempted and killing takes place.

combined cases with sexual assault: cases in which sexual assault occurs in conjunction with robbery, execution, or revenge killing.

execution: cases in which victims are deliberately sought out and murdered, as in a contract or revenge killing.

execution-style: cases in which robbery occurs and victims are tied, blindfolded, etc.

murder: cases that appear to be executions but for which no profit or gangland motive can be established.

murder robbery: cases in which killing occurs and victim is robbed.

robbery execution: cases in which a robbery occurs and victims are deliberately killed without resistance.

robbery homicide or *robbery murder:* cases in which robbery is completed and killing takes place.

sex: cases in which sexual assault appears to be the primary motive.

TERMS RELATED TO NON-FELONY CASES

attempted robbery, extortion: includes cases in which perpetrator was killed by intended victim in felony case.

murder: includes cases in which there was some premeditation but which lack sufficient planning, situational type or information to be classified as execution.

police shooting: cases in which perpetrator was shot by public or private police.

social conflict: includes acquaintances or strangers in arguments.

social conflict, close relationship: includes arguments between family, cohabs or friends that result in killings.

Bibliography

Athens, Lonnie H. "The Self and the Violent Criminal Act." *Urban Life and Culture*, 3(1977):98–112.

———. *Violent Criminal Acts and Actors: A Symbolic Interactionist Study.* Boston: Oxford Press, 1980.

Avison, Neville H. "Victims of Homicide." In *Victimology: A New Focus*, edited by Israel Drapkin and Emileo Viano. Lexington, Mass.: D. C. Heath, 1975. Pp. 55–68.

Becker, Howard. "Problems of Inference and Proof in Participant Observation," Reprinted in *Qualitative Methodology*, edited by William J. Filstead. Chicago: Markham Publishing Co., 1970. Pp. 189–201.

Block, Richard. *Violent Crime: Environment, Interaction and Death.* Lexington, Mass.: D. C. Heath, 1977.

Boudouris, James. "A Classification of Homicides." *Criminology*, 3(1974):525–40.

———. *Trends in Homicide in Detroit 1926–1968.* Unpublished Ph.D. dissertation, Wayne State University, Detroit, Mich., 1971.

Brown, Claude. *Manchild in the Promised Land.* New York: Macmillan, 1965.

Browning, C. H. "Handguns and Homicide: A Public Health Problem." *Journal of the American Medical Association*, 236(November 1976):2198–2200.

California Department of Justice. "Homicide in California, 1973." Sacramento, Calif., 1974.

Camp, George M. *Nothing to Lose: A Study of Bank Robbery in America.* Unpublished Ph.D. dissertation, Yale University, New Haven, Conn., 1968.

Capote, Truman. *In Cold Blood.* New York: Signet Books, 1965.

Charon, Joel M. *Symbolic Interactionism: An Introduction, An Interpretation, An Integration.* Englewood Cliffs, N.J.: Prentice-Hall, 1979.

Clinard, Marshall B., and Abbott, D. J. *Crime in Developing Countries.* New York: Wiley, 1973.

Cloward, Richard A., and Ohlin, Lloyd E. *Delinquency and Opportunity.* New York: Free Press, 1960.

Cohn, Alvin. *Crime and Justice Administration.* Philadelphia: J. B. Lippincott, 1976.

Cole, K. E., et al. "Women Who Kill: A Sociopsychological Study." *Archives of General Psychology,* 19(1968): 1–8.

Conklin, John E. *Robbery and the Criminal Justice System.* Philadelphia: J. B. Lippincott, 1972.

Curtis, Lynn. *Criminal Violence.* Lexington, Mass.: D. C. Heath, 1974.

DeBaun, Everett. "The Heist: The Theory and Practice of Armed Robbery." *Harper's* (February 1950), pp. 69–77.

Deutscher, Irwin. "Evil Companions and Naughty Behavior: Some Thoughts and Evidence Bearing on a Folk Hypothesis." In *Deviance,* edited by Jack Douglas and Robert Scott. New York: Basic Books, 1969.

Dietz, Mary L. *Violence and Control: A Study of Some Relationships of the Violent Subculture to the Control of Interpersonal Violence.* Unpublished Ph.D. dissertation, Wayne State University, 1968.

————. "The Violent Subculture: The Genesis of Violence." In *Violence in Canada,* edited by Mary Alice Beyer Gammon. Toronto: Methuen, 1978.

Douglas, Jack D. *Investigative Social Research.* Beverly Hills, Calif.: Sage Publications, 1976.

Einstader, Werner J. *Armed Robbery: A Career Study in Perspective.* Unpublished Ph.D. dissertation, University of California, 1966.

————. "Contingencies and Risk in Criminalization: On Becoming a Systematic Robber." In *Images of Crime: Offenders and Victims,* edited by T. P. Thornberry and Edward Sagarin. New York: Praeger, 1974.

————. "The Social Organization of Armed Robbery." *Social Problems (1969), 64–83.*

Feeney, Floyd, and Weir, Adriane. "The Prevention and Control of Robbery." Center on Administration of Criminal Justice, University of California–Davis, 1975.

Firearm Use in Violent Crime. A selected bibliography compiled by Marla Wilson Ray, Robert N. Brenner, and Marjorie Kravitz. National Institute of Law Enforcement and Criminal Justice, 1978.

Fisher, Dave (with Joey). *Hit #29.* New York: Pocket Books, 1975.

————. *Killer: Autobiography of a Mafia Hit Man.* New York: Pocket Books, 1973.

Fisher, Joseph C. "Homicide in Detroit: The Role of Firearms." *Criminology,* 14(1976):387–400.

Glaser, Barney, and Strauss, Anselm. "Awareness Contexts and Social Interaction." *American Sociological Review,* 29(1964):669–79.

Goffman, Erving. *The Presentation of Self in Everyday Life.* New York: Doubleday, 1959.

————. *Encounters.* Indianapolis: Bobbs-Merrill, 1961.

Hare, A. Paul. *The Handbook of Small Group Research.* 2nd ed. New York: Free Press, 1976.

Harris, Richard D. "Homicide in Detroit 1970–1973: A Test of the Subculture of Violence Hypothesis." Unpublished Ph.D. dissertation, Wayne State University, 1976.

Hartung, Frank. *Crime, Law and Society.* Detroit: Wayne State University Press, 1965.

Haskell, Martin R. and Yablonsky, Lewis. *Crime and Delinquency.* 3rd ed. Chicago: Rand McNally, 1978.

Hewitt, John P. *Self and Society: A Symbolic Interactionist Social Psychology.* Boston: Allyn and Bacon, 1976.

Horrocks, John E., and Jackson, Dorothy W. *Self and Role: A Theory of Self Process and Role Behavior.* Boston: Houghton-Mifflin, 1972.

Irwin, John. *The Felon.* Englewood Cliffs, N.J.: Prentice-Hall, 1970.

Jaywardene, C. H. S. *The Penalty of Death.* Lexington, Mass.: D. C. Heath, 1978.

Klienke, Chris L. *Self Perception: The Psychology of Personal Awareness.* San Francisco: W. H. Freeman, 1978.

Letkeman, Peter. *Crime as Work.* Englewood Cliffs, N.J.: Prentice-Hall, 1973.

Levi, Kenneth J. "Icemen: Detroit Killers in a Conflict Model." Unpublished Ph.D. dissertation, University of Michigan–Ann Arbor, 1975.

Luckenbill, David F. "Other People's Lives: The Social Organization of Criminal Homicide." Unpublished M.A. thesis, University of California–Santa Barbara, 1974.

———. "Criminal Homicide as a Situated Transaction." *Social Problems,* 25(1977)2: 176–86.

Lundsgaarde, Harold. *Murder in Space City.* New York: Oxford Univ. Press, 1977.

McCall, George J., and Simmons, J. L. *Identities and Interactions.* Rev. ed. New York: Free Press, 1978.

Milgrim, S. "Group Pressure and Action Against a Person." *Journal of Abnormal and Social Psychology,* 69(1964):137–43.

Miller, Gale. *Odd Jobs.* Englewood Cliffs, N.J.: Prentice-Hall, 1978.

Ministry of the Solicitor General, Research and Statistics Development Board. "Statistics Relating to the Gun Control Question." Ottawa, March 1976.

Pearson, John. *The Profession of Violence: The Rise and Fall of the Kray Twins.* London: Weidenfield and Nicholson, 1972.

Polsky, Howard W. *Cottage Six.* New York: Russell Sage Foundation, 1972.

Prus, Robert C. "From Barrooms to Bedrooms: Toward a Theory of Interpersonal Violence." In *Violence in Canada,* edited by Mary Alice Beyer Gammon. Toronto: Methuen, 1978.

Radzinowicz, Sir Leon, and King, John. *The Growth of Crime: The International Experience.* New York: Basic Books, 1977.

Reed, Paul; Blyzinski, Theresa; and Gaucher, Robert. "Homicide in Canada: A Statistical Synopsis." In *Violence in Canada,* edited by Mary Alice Beyer Gammon. Toronto: Methuen, 1978, pp. 178–208.

Reid, Sue Titus. *Crime and Criminology.* 2nd ed. New York: Holt, Rinehart and Winston, 1979.

Schloss, Barbara, and Giesbrecht, N. A. *Murder in Canada: A Report on Capital and Non-Capital Murder Statistics.* Toronto: Centre of Criminology, 1972.

Sellin, Thorsten. "Homicide in Retentionist and Abolitionist States." In *Capital Punishment*, edited by T. Sellin. New York: Harper and Row, 1967. Pp. 135–38.

Shaw, Marvin E. *Group Dynamics: The Psychology of Small Group Behavior*. New York: McGraw-Hill, 1976.

Sherrill, Robert. *The Saturday Night Special*. New York: Charterhouse, 1973.

Shover, Neal. "Structures and Careers in Burglary," *Journal of Criminal Law, Criminology and Police Sciences*, 63(1972):540–49.

———. "The Social Organization of Burglary." *Social Problems* (Spring 1973), pp. 499–514.

Skogan, Wesley G. "Weapon Use in Robbery." In *Violent Crime: Historical and Contemporary Issues*, edited by James A. Inciardi and Anne E. Pottieger. Beverly Hills, Calif.: Sage Publications, 1978.

Smith, Vern E. "Detroit's Heroin Subculture." *Newsweek*, 1972.

———. *The Jones Men*. New York: Warner, 1976.

Sykes, G. M., and Matza, D. "Techniques of Neutralization: A Theory of Delinquency." *American Sociological Review* 22(December 1967):664–70.

Thompson. Hunter S. *The Hell's Angels*. New York: Ballantine, 1966.

Turner, Ralph H. "The Role and the Person." *American Journal of Sociology*, 84(1978):1–23.

Uniform Crime Reports, Federal Bureau of Investigation. Washington, D.C.: U.S. Government Printing Office, 1978.

West, D. J.; Roy, C.; and Nichols, F. L. *Understanding Sexual Attacks*. Toronto: Heinemann, 1978.

Wilt, G. Marie. *Toward an Understanding of the Social Realities of Participants in Homicides*. Unpublished Ph.D. dissertation, Wayne State University, Detroit, 1974.

————, and Bannon, James. *A Comprehensive Analysis of Conflict Motivated Homicides and Assaults— Detroit 1972–1973, Final Report.* Washington, D.C.: Police Foundation, 1974.

Wolfgang, M. E., and Ferracuti, F. *The Subculture of Violence: Toward an Integrated Theory of Criminology.* London: Tavistock, 1967.

Yeager, M. G.: Alriani, J. D.; and Loving, N. "How Well Does the Handgun Protect You and Your Family." U.S. Conference of Mayors, Technical Report no. 2, Washington, D.C., 1976.

Yokelson, Samuel, and Samenow, Stanton E. *The Criminal Personality.* Vol. 1. New York: Jason Aronson, 1976.

Zimring, F. E. "Determinants of Death Rate from Robbery—A Detroit Time Study." *Journal of Legal Studies,* 1(1977):317–32.

————. "Getting Serious about Guns." *The Nation,* 214(1922):457–61.

Index

227